NEW & NATURAL
FRUIT

Pamela Westland

BELL & HYMAN

First published 1985 by
Bell & Hyman Limited
Denmark House
37-39 Queen Elizabeth Street
London SE1 2QB

Cover photograph by Rob Matheson
Cover design by Norman Reynolds
ISBN 0 7135 2524 X

British Library Cataloguing in Publication Data
Westland, Pamela
Fruit.
1, Cookery (Fruit)
I. Title
641.6'4 TX811

Typeset by Typecast Ltd., Maidstone.
Printed and bound by the Pitman Press Ltd; Bath.

CONTENTS

Acknowledgements

The author and publishers would like to thank the following for supplying photographs.

The California Raisin Advisory Board (facing page 24)
The Summer Orange Office (facing page 25)
McDougall's Flour (facing page 48)
National Dairy Council (facing page 49)

INTRODUCTION

If you set a team of food technologists and marketing experts the task of packaging a range of essential nutrients and valuable dietary fibre, they couldn't possibly come up with anything nearly as delicious and utterly irresistible as fresh and dried fruits.

Gather blackberries from the hedgerow one dewy autumn day and you are filling your basket with vitamin C — high in all soft fruits — potassium, so important to the functioning of body cells, and, because of all the pips, fibre that hastens the passage of food through the body. Slice a russet-coloured Comice pear into a fruit salad and you are adding fruit sugars, carbohydrate, potassium and other mineral salts, trace elements, vitamins A and C and — as long as you leave the skin intact — some fibre. Serve roast poultry with cranberries, one of the gifts the American Indians brought to the Pilgrims, and in that glistening, glowing red spoonful there is, besides the sugars and vitamins, salt, potassium, calcium, magnesium, phosphates, iron, copper, sulphure, chloride and carotene. Who'd have thought it!

With our new enthusiasm for healthy straight-from-the-farm foods, you might think we were discovering the nutritional values of fruits for the very first time. Not so! Apples, which have been bred over the centuries from the indigenous wild fruit, crabapples, known as wildings, were recognized by Gerard, the sixteenth-century herbalist, as 'good for a hot stomach'. Though he's a comparatively modern preacher. Carbonized samples of apples found in Italian and Swiss lake dwellings may be as much as 15,000 years old. Pears, described in Homer's Odyssey as 'one of the gifts of the gods' have been cultivated for over 3,000 years. And dried fruits were held in such high esteem by the kings of ancient Egypt that they were often among the treasures buried in the tombs.

Which is not surprising. For dried fruits have all the healthy virtues of fresh fruits — only more so. The process of drying, whether it is by the age-old means of exposure to the wind and sun or by modern controlled-heat methods in hot-air cabinets, evaporates the water in the fruit. After processing this can leave the fruit with a moisture content as low as 20 per cent, a state which discourages the growth of harmful organisms and deterioration.

Indeed, drying is *the* perfect means of preserving fruit, discovered probably by accident in ancient times but now, on health grounds, to be infinitely preferred to canning in sugary syrup. Dried fruits, from plump golden raisins to blue-black prunes, are concentrated packages of nutrients; the very essence, so to speak, of their fresh counterparts. Only a small amount of vitamin C — never in any case likely to be lacking in a Western diet — is lost in the process.

Once so much of the water is eliminated, the proportion of dietary fibre is increased many-fold. More than ten-fold, in fact. Fresh apricots, for example, contain 2.1 per cent fibre, the dried fruit — sun-gold and delicious — 24 per cent. Black grapes have a minimal 0.3 per cent fibre whilst raisins clock up 6.8 per cent.

Packed as they are with 'goodness', dried fruits are the natural and obvious way to cut down on refined sugars and artificial sweeteners. Indeed, dried dates, a heady 63.9 per cent of which are natural fruit sugars, can be made into a brown sugar look-alike.

To make this, dry stoned dates at the lowest oven temperture overnight, until they feel half as heavy. Then grind them a few at a time in a blender or food processor. A spoonful of this 'sugar' has all the fruit's original nutrients and 8.7 per cent fibre.

Fresh or dried, fruits are one of the most versatile of foods and, thanks in no small part to their health properties, are firmly established in the traditional regional cultures around the world. The acidity of fruits is of particular value to offset the saturated fats of red meat dishes, as in a North African speciality of lamb with dried apricots and a version of Italian osso bucco with gooseberries. In poultry and game which can tend towards dryness, the juiciness of fruits has distinct advantages — pigeon with grapes and chicken with mangoes are tempting examples.

Swift transport and improved storage facilities have brought fresh fruits from far-away places within reach of most of us. Alongside home-grown apples, pears, plums and familiar citrus fruits we can now, as the seasons come round, buy kiwi fruits, lychees, pomegranates, papayas, dates, Cape gooseberries, figs, cranberries and ugli to name a few. A harvest of almost unbounded fruitfulness! Throughout the book you will find details of how to prepare less familiar fruits and ideas to serve them — often simply and at their best.

And from breakfast, when it's definitely 'go to work on a plate of fruit', through first courses, salads, main dishes, desserts and traditional baking you will find fruit, that genius of nutritious packaging, in some 150 delicious and, I hope, utterly irresistible ways.

Breakfast

How anyone used to go off to work or school full of vim and vigour after one of the those groaning-sideboard breakfasts of kidneys, kippers, kedgeree and the like, I never could imagine.

Today's trend couldn't be more different. Now we start the day on something that's quick and easy to prepare, can be eaten comfortably with an eye on the clock and is, above all, nourishing. And dried and fresh fruits, full of vitamins, have a vitally important part to play in this new-look vitality food.

Half-slices of bacon wrapped round fresh apples or dried apricots; kebabs of smoked fish and citrus fruits; a fluffy omelette speckled with crisp, cubed fruit, and open sandwiches of glowing golden and cool green fruits — they're all a far cry from greasy plates laden with burdensome calories. There are mix-and-match recipes for muesli, fruit and yoghurt concoctions and tangy salads — all temptingly appetizing and sure to get you off to a good start.

Buckwheat Muesli

Serves 4

4 level tblsp toasted buckwheat
¼ pt (150 ml) unsweetened white grape juice
4 level tblsp rolled oats
1 level tblsp wheatgerm
2 oz (50 g) brazils, roughly chopped
4 oz (100 g) seedless grapes
2 level tblsp dried mulberries
2 dessert apples, cored and thinly sliced
plain low-fat yoghurt, to serve

1. Soak the buckwheat in the grape juice for 2-3 hours.
2. Stir in the remaining ingredients and serve with yoghurt.

Orange and Date Muesli

Serves 4

4 oz (100 g) rolled oats
2 level tblsp oatbran and oatgerm
1 level tblsp sunflower seeds
2 level tblsp hazelnuts
1 oz (25 g) sultanas
3 oz (75 g) dates, chopped
1 oz (25 g) fig paste, chopped
¾ pt (425 ml) buttermilk
¼ pt (150 ml) plain low-fat yoghurt
juice of 1 orange
1 level tsp finely grated orange rind
2 oranges, segmented

1. Mix together the cereals, seeds, nuts and dried fruits. This mixture can be stored in an airtight container.
2. Beat together the buttermilk, yoghurt, orange juice and grated rind, and chill.
3. Serve the muesli with the buttermilk mixture and topped with fresh orange segments.

Muesli Flake

Serves 4

3 oz (75 g) rolled oats
1 oz (25 g) barley flakes
1 oz (25 g) wheat flakes
2 oz (50 g) dried apple flakes
2 level tblsp dried prune flakes
1 oz (25 g) dried banana chips
2 dessert apples, cored and thinly sliced
2 oz (50 g) fresh blackberries, if available
2 level tblsp orange juice
buttermilk to serve

1. Mix together all the dry ingredients, which can be stored in an airtight container.
2. Toss the apple slices and blackberries, if available, in the orange juice.
3. Serve the muesli with buttermilk and top with the fresh apples and blackberries.

* Once you take a liking to a particular muesli mix, it makes time-and-trouble sense to make it up in larger quantities and store.

Blackberry Fool Yoghurt

Serves 4

½ pt (275 ml) blackberry purée
1 pt (575 ml) plain low-fat yoghurt
3 level tblsp wheatgerm
2 level tblsp clear honey
4 oz (100 g) fresh blackberries

1. Beat together the blackberry purée, yoghurt and wheatgerm.
2. Serve the mixture chilled. Top each portion with a drizzle of honey and the fresh berries.

Apricot and Almond Yoghurt

Serves 4

½ pt (275 ml) thick dried apricot purée
4 level tblsp flaked almonds
3 oz (75 g) dried apricots, chopped
1 pt (575 ml) plain low-fat yoghurt
4 level tblsp muesli

1. Stir together the apricot purée and almonds. Stir the chopped apricots into the yoghurt.
2. In individual glasses, make layers of the purée and the yoghurt. Sprinkle the muesli on top.

Banana Reveille

Serves 2

¾ pt (425 ml) plain low-fat yoghurt
2 medium bananas, sliced
8-12 dried apricots, soaked and drained
2 eggs
1 level tblsp clear honey
a pinch of ground cinnamon
1 level tblsp muesli, to decorate

1. Put all the ingredients except the muesli into a blender and liquidize until smooth. Chill. Pour into drinking glasses and sprinkle with the muesli to decorate.

* Serve this refreshing and vitalizing fruit concoction as a breakfast or mid-morning drink. Or pour it over muesli, sliced fresh fruits such as peaches and apples, or soft fruits like blackberries.

Dried Fruit Variety

Serves 4

1 lb (450 g) mixed dried fruits — apple rings, apricots, figs, peaches and pears
juice and thinly pared rind of 1 lemon
a pinch of ground cinnamon
4 level tblsp slivered almonds
plain low-fat yoghurt, to serve

1. Soak the fruit in water to cover for 2-3 hours, or overnight.
2. Add the lemon juice and rind and cinnamon, bring to the boil, cover and simmer for 45 minutes. Cool, remove the strips of lemon rind and chill.
3. Sprinkle on the almonds and serve with yoghurt.

For still more variety, add 1 orange, peeled and very thinly sliced, to the dried fruit for the last 5 minutes of cooking time.

Apple and Prune Dominoes

Serves 4

8 oz (225 g) prunes
6 oz (150 g) dried apple rings
½ pt (275 ml) unsweetened cloudy apple juice
8 oz (225 g) low-fat cottage cheese
1 level tblsp flaked almonds

1. Soak the prunes in water for 2-3 hours. Poach them in the liquid for 30 minutes, or until tender. Drain them, split and — if time — remove stones.
2. Soak the apple rings in the apple juice for 1 hour. Poach the fruit in the liquid for 15 minutes. Do not allow the rings to break up.
3. Add the prunes to the apple rings, cool and chill. You can prepare the fruit to this stage the day before.
4. Top the fruit with teaspoons of cottage cheese and scatter with the almonds.

Citrus Salad

Serves 4

2 oranges, segmented
2 grapefruit, segmented
4 oz (100 g) dried apricots, soaked and drained
1 level tblsp mint leaves
½ pt (275 ml) plain low-fat yoghurt
1 level tblsp very thinly sliced orange peel,
mint sprigs, to decorate

1. Mix together the fruit and mint leaves and stir in the yoghurt.
2. Decorate with the orange strips and mint sprigs. Serve chilled.

Open Sandwiches

Makes 8

8 slices black rye bread, pumpernickel or crispbread
12 oz (350 g) low-fat cottage cheese
2 oranges, thinly sliced into rings
1 mango, peeled, stoned and sliced
2 level tblsp walnut halves
1 box salad cress
2 kiwi fruits, peeled and thinly sliced into rings
1 bunch watercress
2 level tblsp pumpkin seeds

1. Have the toppings ready prepared and assemble just before serving. Spread each slice with cottage cheese.

2. On 4 slices arrange a pattern of orange slices and mango wedges and scatter with walnuts. Decorate with tiny bunches of cress.
3. On the 4 remaining slices, arrange slices of kiwi fruits and watercress sprigs and scatter with pumpkin seeds.

Apple and Cheese Layer

Serves 4

4 large cooking apples, peeled and cored
2 level tsp clear honey, melted
8 oz (225 g) low-fat cottage cheese, sieved
4 level tblsp thick dried apricot purée
1 level tblsp chopped hazelnuts
wholemeal toast, to serve

1. Cut each apple across into 4 rings. Cover the grill pan with foil.
2. Brush one side of the apple slices with honey and grill until bubbling.
3. Mix together the sieved cheese and apricot purée. Turn the apple slices, spread with the cheese mixture and grill.
4. Reassemble the apples, sprinkle the tops with nuts and grill for 1 minute. Serve with toast.

Apricot Sizzlers

Serves 4

8 rashers back bacon
16 dried apricots, soaked and drained
4 oz (100 g) button mushrooms
4 bay leaves
wholemeal toast, to serve

1. Cut the rind from the bacon. Cut each rasher in half and 'stretch' it by stroking it firmly along a board, using the back of a knife.
2. Place an apricot at one end of each bacon piece and roll up to enclose the fruit.
3. Cut the stalks from the mushrooms. Thread the bacon rolls, mushrooms and bay leaves on to 4 skewers.
4. Grill for about 5 minutes under medium heat, turning the skewers frequently. Serve with hot toast.

* You can substitute soaked and pitted prunes for the dried apricots.

Kidney Kebabs

Serves 4

4 rashers streaky bacon
2 small cooking apples, peeled, cored and quartered
6 lamb's kidneys, peeled, halved and cored
4 pieces wholemeal pitta

1. Cut the rind from the bacon, halve each slice and 'stretch' it by scraping it firmly with the back of a knife. Wrap a piece of bacon around each quarter of apple.
2. Thread kidney halves and the bacon and apple rolls on to 4 skewers, starting and ending with kidney.
3. Grill the skewers under medium heat for about 5 minutes, turning them frequently. Serve each one in a piece of warmed pitta.

Mackerel and Grapefruit Sticks

Serves 4

4 smoked mackerel fillets
2 grapefruit, segmented
1 orange, segmented
1 level tblsp chopped mint
1 level tblsp vegetable oil
3 level tblsp orange juice
pepper

1. Cut each mackerel fillet into 4. Thread on to 4 skewers with the grapefruit and orange segments.
2. Mix together the mint, oil, orange juice and pepper. Pour over the skewers, cover and leave in the refrigerator for at least 1 hour – or overnight if that's easier.
3. Grill the skewers under medium heat for 4-5 minutes, turning frequently. Serve with hot wholemeal rolls.

Orchard Omelette

Serves 4

½ oz (15 g) margarine
2 small cooking apples, peeled, cored and diced
2 medium potatoes, cooked and diced
2 rashers streaky bacon, rinded and cut into 1 inch (2.5 cm) squares
6 eggs
salt and pepper
2 level tblsp water
1 dessert apple, cored and thinly sliced, to garnish

1. Melt the magarine in a large non-stick omelette pan and fry the cooking apple, potato and bacon over medium heat for 4-5 minutes, stirring frequently.
2. Beat together the eggs, salt, pepper and water. Pour into the pan and, using a spatula, continually draw the cooked egg mixture from the sides of the pan into the middle. When the underside is firm and the top still runny, cook under a hot grill until the top is just set.
3. Cut into 4 wedges and serve topped with the apple slices.

Crunchy Muesli Bars

Makes 12 bars

6 oz (175 g) muesli base
2 oz (50 g) seedless raisins
2 oz (50 g) chopped hazelnuts
6 level tblsp sunflower oil
4 level tblsp clear honey

1. Mix together the muesli, raisins and nuts.
2. Melt the oil and honey over low heat.
3. Pour the honey mixture into the dry ingredients and mix well.
4. Pour the mixture into a greased 7 x 9 inch (21 x 27 cm) baking tin and level the top.
5. Bake in the oven at 375°F (190°C) Gas 5 for 30 minutes.
6. Leave the tin on a wire rack to cool. Mark out into bars and cut when cold. Store in an airtight tin.

FIRST COURSES

Fruit, light, tangy and refreshing, gets any meal off to a healthy and appetizing start. Whether it is simply half a chilled grapefruit meticulously prepared and garnished with grapes or cherries, or a classic combination like avocado pears piled high with piquant prawns, fruit is firmly established as a favourite introductory course.

Make the most of luxury fruits which have a short season such as fresh figs, kiwi fruits, or persimmons with their star-shaped seed pattern, by serving them simply sliced with Parma or other hams, smoked fish, or cold meats. Alternate slices of these showy fruits with melon, grapefruit or avocado for economy. And give more familiar fruits a new zing — two-tone melon soup, melon in curry sauce or with raspberries, piping hot grilled grapefruit, and avocado baked with crab are among our suggestions.

Curried Melon Scoops

Serves 4

1 ripe cantaloupe melon
½ pt (275 ml) plain low-fat yoghurt
2 level tsp curry paste
1 level tsp mango sauce
1 level tsp orange juice
mint sprigs, to garnish

1. Halve the melon, remove the seeds and scoop out the flesh, using a vegetable baller.
2. Beat together the yoghurt, curry paste, sauce and orange juice.
3. Toss the melon in the yoghurt sauce, cover and chill for at least 30 minutes. Garnish with the mint sprigs.

Parma Ham and Figs

Serves 4

Fresh figs are available for such a short season, in the autumn, that they are always a luxury. Serve and present them at their best — simply halved.

12 fresh figs — black, green or golden, as available
6 oz (175 g) Parma or other cured and uncooked ham, sliced wafer-thin
a few watercress sprigs, to garnish
1 lemon, quartered

1. Leave the figs in a warm room or in the sun in order to serve them slightly warm. Remove the stalks and slice the figs in half lengthways, to show off the seed colour to advantage.
2. Arrange the ham on individual plates with the fig slices in a decorative pattern. Garnish with a very little watercress and the wedge of lemon. Some people find that the juice brings out the full flavour of the figs. Serve with thinly sliced wholemeal bread.

Brie Pears

Serves 4

4 large cooking pears
1 large bay leaf
1 level tsp lemon juice
¼ pt (150 ml) plain low-fat yoghurt
2 oz (50 g) Brie
2 level tblsp parsley (flat-leafed variety if available), chopped
pepper
spinach leaves, to serve
2 level tblsp walnut halves

1. Peel the pears, leaving on the stalks. Scoop out the cores, using a small sharp knife.
2. Cover the pears with water, add the bay leaf and lemon juice and poach for 15 minutes, or until they are tender. Drain them, pat dry with kitchen paper and leave to cool.
3. Liquidize the yoghurt and Brie in a blender. Stir in the parsley and season with pepper.
4. Line a dish with the spinach leaves. Arrange the pears to stand upright. Pour the sauce over them and scatter with the walnuts just before serving.

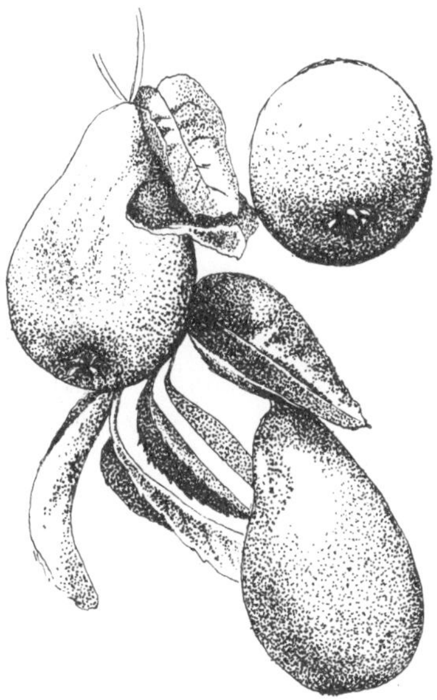

Sunset Melon
Serves 4

1 honeydew melon
8 oz (225 g) fresh or frozen raspberries
juice and grated rind of ½ orange
herb leaves, as available, to decorate

1. Cut the melon in quarters, discard the seeds and cut the flesh away from the rind. Cut the fruit into ¾ inch (2 cm) cubes.
2. Liquidize and then sieve the raspberries to make a purée. Stir in the orange juice and rind.
3. Pour the raspberry sauce over the melon cubes, stir well, cover and chill. Decorate the dish with scented geranium or bay leaves, if you have them.

Grilled Grapefruit
Serves 4

2 large grapefruit, halved
4 level tblsp sultanas
2 level tblsp medium sherry
a pinch of ground ginger
1 level tsp melted butter

1. Slice through the grapefruit segments to separate them and remove the central core.
2. Mix the sultanas, sherry and ginger and pack into the grapefuit centres.
3. Drizzle the butter over the fruit. Grill under medium heat for 5 minutes. Serve hot.

Baked Avocado with Crab

Serves 4

7 fl oz (200 ml) plain low-fat yoghurt
2 medium eggs
4 level tblsp grated Parmesan cheese
8 oz (225 g) crabmeat, flaked
1 level tsp curry powder
1 level tsp tomato paste
salt and pepper
2 large avocados, halved and stoned

1. Beat together the yoghurt, eggs, half the cheese, the crabmeat, curry powder and tomato paste and season with salt and pepper.
2. Pile the mixture into the avocado halves and sprinkle the remaining cheese on top.
3. Place the pears on a baking sheet. Bake in the oven at 350°F (180°C), Gas 4 for 20-25 minutes, until the filling is set and crisp on top. Serve at once, with thinly sliced wholemeal bread.

Apricot and Cucumber Soup

Serves 4

6 oz (175 g) dried apricots
1½ pt (850 ml) chicken stock
1 orange
1 medium cucumber
1 medium onion, finely chopped
1 level tblsp vegetable oil
2 level tsp curry powder
salt and pepper
2 level tblsp pumpkin seeds, to garnish

1. Soak the apricots in the stock with the thinly pared orange rind for 2-3 hours. Add the orange juice and simmer for 45 minutes.
2. Cut 8 thin slices from the cucumber, for garnish. Peel and roughly chop the remainder.
3. Fry the onion in the oil over medium heat for 3-4 minutes, stirring once or twice. Stir in the curry powder and chopped cucumber and cook for 2 minutes.
4. Liquidize the apricots with the stock and the cucumber mixture. Return to the pan and heat gently. Season well with salt and pepper.
5. Serve the soup garnished with floating slices of cucumber topped with the pumpkin seeds.

Black rye bread is a good accompaniment.

Artichoke Soup

Serves 6

1 large onion, sliced
1 lb (450 g) Jerusalem artichokes, peeled and sliced
8 oz (225 g) carrots, sliced
1¾ pt (1 litre) chicken stock
1 orange
salt and pepper
6 level tsp soured cream, to garnish

1. Simmer the onion, artichokes and carrots in the stock for 10 minutes.
2. Add the unpeeled orange, cut into segments, and simmer for a further 10 minutes. Remove a few carrot slices for garnish.
3. Cut flowers or other shapes from the reserved carrot slices. (A small aspic cutter is useful here.)
4. Liquidize the soup in a blender. Return to the pan and reheat.
5. Stir 1 level tsp soured cream into each portion and garnish with the carrot flowers.

Pershore Plum Soup

Serves 4

2 lb (900 g) cooking plums
½ pt (275 ml) water
½ pt (275 ml) red wine
2 level tblsp clear honey
2 inch (5 cm) stick cinnamon
2 level tblsp lemon juice
1 level tblsp cornflour
½ pt (275 ml) buttermilk
2 level tblsp toasted sesame seeds, to garnish

1. Simmer the plums, water, wine, honey, cinnamon and lemon juice for 20 minutes. Remove the cinnamon and sieve the fruit and liquid.

2. Blend the cornflour with 2 level tblsp water, stir in a little of the purée and then return it all to the pan. Stir in the buttermilk and bring slowly to the boil, stirring constantly, until the soup thickens.

3. Serve the soup hot, garnished with the sesame seeds. Matzo biscuits are a good accompaniment.

* As a delicious alternative, substitute pitted black cherries for the plums, reserving 4 bunches for garnish.

Iced Orange and Avocado Soup

Serves 4

1 avocado
1 small onion, finely chopped
1 garlic clove, chopped
½ pt (275 ml) chicken stock
2 oranges
salt and pepper
¼ pt (150 ml) plain low-fat yoghurt
¼ pt (150 ml) frozen concentrated orange juice, thawed

1. Halve and stone the avocado and scoop out the flesh. Simmer it for 5 minutes with the onion and garlic in the stock.

2. Very thinly pare the orange rind and cut it into fine shreds. Reserve for garnish.

3. Peel the oranges and discard the seeds. Liquidize the orange flesh with the avocado and stock. Season well with salt and pepper. Cool.

4. Beat the avocado mixture with the yoghurt and orange juice and whisk well. Chill. Garnish with the orange strips to serve.

Frosted Yoghurt Soup

Serves 4

8 oz (225 g) strawberries
2 level tblsp lemon juice
1 pt (575 ml) plain low-fat yoghurt, chilled
½ small cucumber, finely chopped
2 level tblsp cider vinegar
2 level tblsp chopped mint
salt and pepper
4 mint sprigs, to garnish

1. Reserve 2 large strawberries for decoration. Mash the rest with the lemon juice and stir into half the yoghurt.
2. Mix the cucumber, vinegar and mint into the remaining yoghurt and season with salt and pepper.
3. In 4 flat serving dishes swirl portions of the strawberry and the cucumber mixtures to make fondant-coloured sections. Don't overdo it and stir the whole lot together!
4. Cut the reserved strawberries in half. Garnish each bowl with a half-strawberry and a mint sprig. Serve chilled.

Chilled Lemon Soup

Serves 4

1½ pt (850 ml) chicken stock
½ pt (275 ml) dry cider
2 oz (50 g) brown short-grain rice
salt and pepper
juice and grated rind of 2 lemons
2 eggs, separated
2 level tblsp snipped chives
4 thin slices lemon, to garnish

1. Simmer the stock, cider and rice in a covered pan with salt, pepper and the lemon rind for 40 minutes. Liquidize in a blender and return to the pan.
2. Mix the lemon juice and egg yolks, beat in a little of the soup and return to the pan. Simmer so very gently that the mixture won't curdle. Cool, skim any fat from the surface — mop up the last remnants with absorbent kitchen paper — and chill.
3. Whisk the egg whites and float, like snowy islands, on top. Scatter on the chives and garnish each chilled bowl with a slice of lemon.

Serve with melba toast.

Banana Dip with Fruit Crudités

Serves 4

3 medium bananas
12 oz (350 g) cottage cheese
¼ pt (150 ml) plain low-fat yoghurt
2 level tblsp mango chutney, chopped
1 level tsp mild curry powder
2 level tblsp sultanas
1 lemon, quartered

Crudités
3 dessert apples, cored and thinly sliced
2 firm pears, peeled, cored and thinly sliced
3 level tblsp lemon juice
4 stalks tender celery, cut into fingers
2 medium carrots, cut into matchstick strips

1. Liquidize all the ingredients for the dip except the sultanas, then stir them in.
2. Toss the apples and pears in lemon juice.
3. Garnish the dip with the lemon wedges and surround it on a plate with the crudités.

Grapefruit, Avocado and Prawn Medley

Serves 4

2 large pink grapefruit, segmented
1 avocado, halved, stoned, peeled and sliced
1 dessert apple, cored and thinly sliced
2 level tblsp lemon juice
4 oz (100 g) peeled prawns
½ bunch watercress sprigs, to garnish

Dressing
2 level tblsp vegetable oil
1 level tblsp red wine vinegar
salt
a pinch of cayenne
1 level tsp clear honey

1. Mix together the dressing ingredients to dissolve the honey.
2. Make a ring of grapefruit segments round a plate. Toss the avocado and apple slices in the lemon juice. Make a ring of alternating avocado and apple slices inside the grapefruit. Arrange the prawns in the centre.
3. Drizzle the dressing over the salad and arrange the watercress sprigs in a ring around the outside. Serve with wholemeal bread.

Double Melon Soup

Serves 6

1 small, ripe cantaloupe melon, peeled, seeded and chopped
2 level tblsp orange juice
1 level tsp grated orange rind
2 level tblsp sweet sherry
½ ripe honeydew melon, peeled, seeded and chopped
2 level tblsp lemon juice
3 level tblsp chopped mint
mint sprigs, to garnish

1. Liquidize the cantaloupe melon with the orange juice and rind and the sherry, cover and chill for at least 3 hours.
2. Liquidize the honeydew melon with the lemon juice and mint, cover and chill for at least 3 hours.
3. Pour equal amounts of each melon mixture into chilled serving bowls for a pretty half-orange, half-green effect. Garnish with mint sprigs and serve chilled.

Fruity Gazpacho

Serves 4

1½ lb (775 g) ripe tomatoes, skinned
1 level tblsp lemon juice
½ pt (275 ml) chicken stock
salt and pepper
1 small onion, finely chopped
4 inch (10 cm) piece cucumber, finely chopped
1 yellow pepper, seeded and cut into matchstick strips
2 peaches, skinned, stoned and thinly sliced
1 dessert apple, cored and thinly sliced
4 level tblsp blackberries or other soft fruit
3 level tblsp chopped parsley

1. Liquidize the tomatoes and lemon juice, stir in the stock and season well with salt and pepper.

2. Stir in the vegetables and fruits, cover and chill for 1 hour to allow the flavours to blend.

3. Just before serving, stir in the parsley. Serve with oatcakes.

Orange and Date Muesli (page 12); Dried Fruit Variety (page 14) and Crunchy Muesli Bars (page 16)

Overleaf: Oriental Orange Cocktail (page 68)

MAIN DISHES

There's a long and noble history attached to cooking fruit with meat and fish. A sound one, too. Earlier cultures devised dishes based on 'the fat of the land', making little or no distinction between vegetables and fruits; they were all foods to be gratefully harvested and, where possible, stored until the next crops ripened.

We are by no means the first generation to discover that both fresh and dried fruits are perfect companions to meat and fish. The high acid content of the fruits positively helps to offset rich, fatty and oily foods, enhancing flavour and facilitating digestion.

Go beyond the traditional apple sauce, and try pork cooked with oranges, lemons, dates, apples, apricots and raisins — all together. Raid the store cupboard for dried apricots to cook with lamb, prunes with beef or rabbit, and figs with chicken. Enjoy the tanginess of rhubarb against the heavy-weight personality of mackerel, or poach fillets of trout in orange and lemon. Go ethnic with a Caribbean casserole of fish and plantain, or more sophisticated with plaice wheels and grapes. Fruit makes the choice as confusing as it is exciting!

Vineyard Plaice

Serves 4

4 fillets of plaice
salt and pepper
2 level tblsp lemon juice
4 level tblsp dry white wine
1 bay leaf
8 oz (225 g) seedless grapes, or white grapes, skinned and seeded
2 level tblsp clear honey
1 level tblsp water
1 level tblsp flour
½ pt (275 ml) plain low-fat yoghurt

1. Season the plaice fillets with salt and pepper and a sprinkling of lemon juice and roll them up skin side out. Place them in a greased baking dish, add the remaining lemon juice, the wine and bay leaf and cover with foil.
2. Bake in the oven at 350°F (180°C), Gas 4 for 20-25 minutes.
3. While the fish is cooking simmer the grapes in the honey and water for 5 minutes.
4. Stir the flour into the yoghurt and strain the fish liquor into it, stirring all the time. Bring slowly to the boil, stirring constantly.
5. Pour the sauce over the fish and decorate with the grapes.

Spiced Fish and Plantain Casserole

Serves 4

The sliced plantains are sautéed before being added to the quick-to-cook ingredients in this Ugandan dish.

2 ripe plantains, peeled and thinly sliced
1 oz (25 g) butter
2 green chillies, seeded and finely chopped
1 red chilli, seeded and finely chopped
15 oz (425 g) can tomatoes
2 level tblsp chopped coriander leaves, or parsley
1¼ lb (550 g) cod fillets, skinned
1 level tblsp lime or lemon juice
salt and pepper

1. In a flameproof casserole sauté the plantain slices in the butter over moderate heat for 5 minutes, turning them once. Add the chillies and stir-fry for 1 minute. Add the tomatoes and juice from the can and the chopped herbs, bring to the boil and simmer for 10 minutes.

2. Season the fish with the lime or lemon juice, salt and pepper and place the fillets in the tomato mixture. Spoon the sauce over the fish and cover the dish.
3. Bake in the oven at 375°F (190°C), Gas 5 for 20 minutes, until the fish is just firm and tender. Serve with brown rice.

Trout Fillets in Sousing Drink

Serves 4

4 medium trout, cleaned and gutted
3 level tblsp flour
salt and pepper
3 level tblsp vegetable oil
4 level tblsp tarragon vinegar
4 level tblsp white wine
2 cloves garlic, crushed
1 level tsp green peppercorns, crushed
2 cloves
2 bay leaves, crumbled
grated rind and juice of 2 oranges
grated rind and juice of 2 lemons
1 orange, thinly sliced, to garnish

1. Toss the trout in the flour seasoned with salt and pepper.
2. Fry the fish in the oil over moderate heat for 3-4 minutes on each side and transfer to a serving dish.
3. Mix together all the remaining ingredients, except the orange slices. Pour into the pan, bring to the boil and boil for 3 minutes. Leave to cool.
4. Strain the liquor over the fish, cover and chill overnight. Garnish with the orange slices. Serve with rye bread and salads.

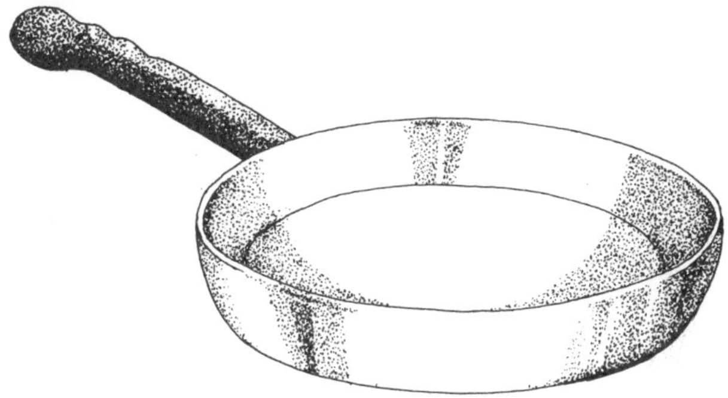

Mackerel with Rhubarb Sauce

Serves 4

4 small mackerel, boned and gutted
½ oz (15 g) butter
1 small onion, chopped
12 oz (350 g) rhubarb
4 oz (100 g) cooked brown rice
½ level tsp crumbled rosemary
salt and pepper
3 level tblsp clear honey
1 level tblsp lemon juice
a pinch of ground cinnamon

1. Melt the butter over moderate heat and fry the onion and 2 sticks of rhubarb, finely chopped. Stir in the rice and rosemary and season with salt and pepper.
2. Stuff the fish with the rice mixture and place in a greased baking dish. Cover with foil.
3. Bake in the oven at 375°F (190°C), Gas 5 for 30-35 minutes.
4. While the fish is cooking, make the sauce. Slice the remaining rhubarb and simmer with the honey, lemon juice and cinnamon. Liquidize or beat to a purée and season with salt and pepper. Serve the sauce separately.

Gingered Prawns

Serves 4

2 level tblsp vegetable oil
4 spring onions, sliced
1 level tsp chopped fresh ginger
1 red pepper, seeded and sliced into matchstick strips
2 small cooking apples, peeled, cored and thinly sliced
12 oz (350 g) peeled prawns

Sauce
2 level tblsp clear honey
1 level tblsp dry sherry
1 level tblsp soy sauce
1 level tblsp cider vinegar
1 level tsp ground ginger
2 level tsp cornflour
2 level tblsp water

1. Mix together all the sauce ingredients; be sure to dissolve the honey.
2. Heat the oil in a large frying-pan or wok. Stir-fry the onions, chopped ginger and pepper over moderately high heat for 1 minute. Add the apples and stir-fry for 1 minute, then the prawns.
3. Immediately pour on the sauce, stir and bring to the boil. Simmer for 1-2 minutes. Serve at once, with rice.

Chicken Breast with Mango

Serves 4

Mangoes are grown in many tropical countries and available fresh almost the year round. The skin may be green, red or yellow, the flesh is bright orange, and surrounds a large flat stone.

4 slices chicken breast, about 5 oz (125 g) each
4 level tblsp green peppercorns, lightly crushed
1 oz (25 g) butter
1 level tsp flour
juice of 1 lime or lemon
4 level tblsp chicken stock
¼ pt (150 ml) soured cream, or plain low-fat yoghurt
salt
1 mango, peeled, stoned and thinly sliced

1. Coat the chicken breasts in the peppercorns.
2. Sauté them in the butter over moderately high heat for 5-6 minutes, turning them once. Remove the chicken and keep it warm.
3. Stir the flour into the pan, then the lime or lemon juice and the stock and bring to the boil, still stirring. Add the cream or yoghurt and season with salt. Heat gently.
4. Pour the sauce on to a dish. Arrange the chicken pieces on top, with a fan of mango slices on each. Serve with a green vegetable such as broccoli spears.

Chicken with Avocado Sauce

Serves 4

4 chicken joints, skinned
1 level tblsp lemon juice
pepper
1 level tsp ground ginger
1 oz (25 g) butter
2 medium onions, thinly sliced
2 level tsp flour
½ pt (275 ml) chicken stock
4 level tblsp soured cream
salt
2 avocados, peeled, stoned and thinly sliced
2 level tblsp blanched almonds, toasted, to garnish

1. Sprinkle the chicken joints with lemon juice and rub in the pepper and ginger. Brown them in a non-stick pan in the butter, turning them frequently, for 5-6 minutes. Remove from the pan.
2. Stir-fry the onions for 2 minutes. Stir in the flour, add the chicken stock and bring to the boil.
3. Return the chicken to the pan, cover and simmer for 45 minutes, until it is tender. Transfer to a serving dish and keep warm. Add the soured cream to the sauce, season with salt and pepper, add the avocado slices and heat gently.
4. Pour the sauce over the chicken and garnish with the almonds.

Hawaiian Chicken

Serves 4

4 chicken joints, skinned
about 4 level tblsp soy sauce
pepper
2 bananas, halved lengthways
1 mango, peeled, stoned and sliced
4 slices pineapple, peeled and cored
1 level tsp ground cinnamon
1 level tblsp melted butter
1 level tblsp lemon juice

1. Brush the chicken joints on all sides with soy sauce and season with pepper. Grill under medium heat for 10 minutes on each side.
2. Place each chicken piece in the centre of a 10 inch (25 cm) square of foil. Surround with banana and mango slices and place a pineapple slice on top. Sprinkle with the cinnamon, butter and lemon juice. Close the foil tightly to make leakproof parcels.
3. Grill for a further 30 minutes, turning the parcels over once. Serve with rice.

* You can chop the remaining pineapple into the rice, or toss it with a green salad accompaniment.

Chicken with Smyrna Figs

Serves 4

4 chicken joints, skinned
1 medium onion, finely chopped
7 fl oz (200 ml) dry cider
1 inch (2.5 cm) piece cinnamon stick
2 level tsp coriander seeds
1 level tblsp clear honey
12 oz (350 g) dried figs, soaked and drained
salt and pepper
2 level tblsp chopped coriander leaves or parsley, to garnish

1. Dry-fry the chicken pieces in a non-stick pan for 5-6 minutes over moderate heat, turning them often.
2. Add the onion and fry for 2 minutes, stirring once or twice.
3. Add the cider, cinnamon, coriander seeds, honey and figs, season with salt and pepper and bring to the boil.
4. Cover and simmer for 40-45 minutes, stirring occasionally, until the chicken is tender. Add a little water if the sauce becomes too dry.
5. Discard the cinnamon. Garnish with the chopped herb. Serve with rice spiced and coloured with turmeric.

Mandarin Risotto

Serves 4

1 medium onion, chopped
2 level tblsp vegetable oil
8 oz (225 g) brown short-grain rice
1 pt (575 ml) chicken stock
12 oz (350 g) cooked chicken, diced
4 oz (100 g) canned water chestnuts, drained, rinsed and thinly sliced
4 oz (100 g) seedless raisins
2 level tblsp soy sauce
grated rind and juice of 1 orange
salt and pepper
4 level tblsp cashew nuts

1. Fry the onion in the oil over moderate heat for 2-3 minutes, stirring once or twice. Stir in the rice for 1 minute. Pour on the stock, bring to the boil, cover and simmer for 40 minutes, stirring once.
2. While the rice is cooking mix together the chicken, water chestnuts, raisins, soy sauce, orange rind and juice and set aside.
3. Stir this mixture into the rice and gently heat through. Season with salt and pepper. Serve hot, garnished with the nuts.

A stir-fried green vegetable such as broccoli spears or mange-tout peas is a good accompaniment.

Marinated Rabbit with Prunes

Serves 4

1 young rabbit, jointed
8 oz (225 g) prunes
¾ pt (425 ml) strained tea
4 oz (100 g) streaky bacon, rind removed, cut into 1 inch (2.5 cm) squares
1 oz (25 g) butter
2 level tblsp flour
¼ pt (150 ml) red wine
¼ pt (150 ml) chicken stock
2 medium carrots, thinly sliced
salt and pepper

Marinade
¼ pt (150 ml) red wine
1 large onion, chopped
2 bay leaves, crumbled
2 level tblsp vegetable oil
6 juniper berries, lightly crushed
a few parsley stalks
1 level tsp dried thyme

1. Mix together the marinade ingredients. Put the rabbit in a strong polythene bag, pour on the marinade and seal the top. Shake well and leave overnight.
2. Soak the prunes overnight in the tea.
3. Remove the rabbit from the marinade and dry thoroughly. Reserve the marinade.
4. Dry-fry the bacon in a non-stick pan until the fat runs. Melt the butter in the pan and brown the rabbit on all sides. Remove it and set aside. Strain the prunes and set aside.
5. Stir in the flour, pour on the strained rabbit marinade, the strained prune liquor, the wine and chicken stock, stirring constantly.
6. Add the rabbit, prunes and carrots and season with salt and pepper. Transfer to a casserole, cover and cook in the oven at 350°F (180°C), Gas 4 for 2 hours, or until the rabbit is tender. Taste and adjust the seasoning.

Serve with wholewheat noodles.

Refectory Rabbit

Serves 4

1 tender, young rabbit, jointed
3 level tblsp flour
salt and pepper
1 level tsp crumbled rosemary
2-3 level tblsp vegetable oil, for frying

Marinade
1 pt (275 ml) sweet red wine
2 level tblsp red wine vinegar
1 level tsp ground ginger
½ level tsp ground cinnamon
1 level tsp clear honey
6 juniper berries, lightly crushed
8 oz (225 g) seedless raisins
4 oz (100 g) dried apricots, halved

1. Mix together all the marinade ingredients. Put the rabbit into a strong polythene bag, pour on the marinade and seal securely. Set aside all day or overnight, turning the bag occasionally if possible.
2. Drain the rabbit, reserving the marinade. Pat the rabbit dry and toss it in the flour seasoned with salt, pepper and rosemary.
3. Fry the rabbit in the oil in a flameproof casserole over moderate heat, turning it frequently to brown it on all sides. Lift out the rabbit, toss it in kitchen paper to remove excess oil and wipe the casserole dry.
4. Return the rabbit to the casserole, pour on the marinade and bring to the boil. Cover and simmer for 1½ hours or until the rabbit is tender. Taste the sauce and adjust the seasoning. Serve with rice.

Pigeons with Grapes

Serves 4

4 plump, young pigeons
2 oz (50 g) softened butter
2 level tsp grated orange rind
salt and pepper
8 slices streaky bacon
8 oz (225 g) button onions or shallots, peeled and whole
7 fl oz (200 ml) dry cider
1 lb (450 g) seedless grapes, or white grapes, skinned and seeded
1 level tblsp flour
¼ pt (150 ml) soured cream, or plain low-fat yoghurt
orange wedges, to garnish

1. Beat the butter and orange rind together. Using half of it, place a small knob inside each bird. Season with salt and pepper. Wrap the pigeons in the bacon slices and tie around with twine.
2. Fry the birds in a flameproof casserole over moderate heat for 15-20 minutes, turning them frequently. Pour off the fat and stir in the onions.
3. Place the pigeons breast side up, pour on the cider, season with salt and pepper, bring to the boil and cover.
4. Cook in the oven at 350°F (180°C) Gas 4 for 1 hour.
5. Add the grapes, cover and cook for a further 20-25 minutes, or until the pigeons are tender. Remove the pigeons and keep them warm.
6. Beat the remaining orange butter into the flour. Add to the sauce and simmer on top of the stove for 3-4 minutes, until the sauce thickens. Stir in the soured cream or yoghurt and adjust the seasoning. Pour over the pigeons and garnish with the orange wedges.

Serve with potatoes boiled in their skins.

Lamb and Apple Parcels
Serves 4

4 lamb shoulder steaks, trimmed of excess fat
grated rind and juice of 1 orange
2 level tblsp chopped mint
1 clove garlic, crushed
½ level tsp mustard powder
½ level tsp ground coriander
a pinch of cayenne
salt and pepper
8 dried apple rings, soaked and drained
about 4 level tsp currants

1. Mix together the orange rind and juice, mint, garlic, mustard, coriander, cayenne, salt and pepper.
2. Grease four 8 inch (20 cm) squares of foil and place a piece of lamb in the centre of each. Place 2 apple rings on each lamb steak and fill the centre with currants.
3. Draw up the sides of the foil, pour on the orange mixture and seal up the parcels securely.
4. Place them on a baking sheet and cook in the oven at 375°F (190°C), Gas 5 for 45 minutes. Increase the heat to 425°F (220°C), Gas 7 and open the foil. Cook for a further 15 minutes.

Cook large jacket potatoes in the oven at the same time.

Glazed Lamb Cutlets with Green Salad
Serves 4

best end of neck of lamb, 8 cutlets, trimmed of excess fat
pepper
1 level tblsp lemon juice

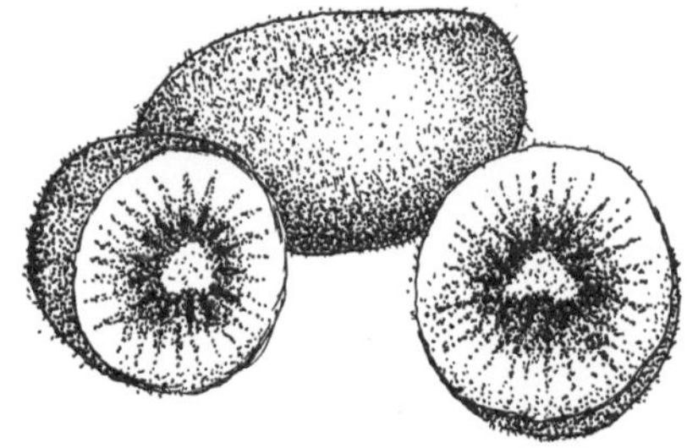

1 kiwi fruit, peeled and thinly sliced
¼ pt (150 ml) aspic jelly, made to the packet instructions
1 level tblsp chopped mint
1 level tblsp medium sherry

Salad
about 8 oz (225 g) Chinese leaves
2 dessert apples, cored and thinly sliced
1 kiwi fruit, peeled, thinly sliced and halved
1 bunch watercress sprigs
2 level tblsp vegetable oil
2 level tsp orange juice
salt and pepper
4 level tblsp seedless raisins

1. Season the lamb with pepper and lemon juice. Roast in the oven at 350°F (180°C), Gas 4 for 50 minutes to 1 hour. Transfer to a wire rack to cool, then slice into cutlets.
2. Mix the aspic jelly with mint and sherry.
3. Place a large dish or tray under the wire rack. Place a slice of kiwi fruit or a pattern made of halves or quarters on each lamb cutlet. Spoon over the jelly to cover the meat and fruit. Leave to chill and set for at least 1 hour.
4. Mix together the Chinese leaves, apple, kiwi fruit, mint and watercress. Mix the oil and orange juice, season with salt and pepper and pour over the salad. Toss well.
5. Arrange the lamb cutlets on a dish with the salad. Scatter the raisins over the salad.

West Country Leg of Lamb

Serves 6–8

3½ lb (1.5 kg) leg of lamb
pepper
8 oz (225 g) button onions or shallots, peeled and whole
4 medium carrots, thickly sliced
2 medium leeks, sliced
2 bay leaves
1 pt (575 ml) chicken stock
salt
6 oz (175 g) currants
1 level tblsp flour
1 level tblsp butter

1. Season the lamb with pepper and place it in a large flameproof casserole. Surround it with the onions, carrots, leeks and bay leaves and pour on the stock. Season with salt and pepper and bring to the boil.
2. Cover the casserole and cook in the oven at 375°F (190°C), Gas 5 for 1 hour.
3. Stir in the currants and cook for a further 45 minutes. Remove the bay leaves.
4. Mix the flour and butter to a paste. Remove the lamb and stir the paste into the sauce. Simmer on top of the stove until it thickens. Adjust the seasoning. Serve the lamb sliced, surrounded by the vegetable and fruit sauce.

Lamb and Pomegranate Rice

Serves 4

Pomegranates, those large, round sunset-coloured fruits, have translucent and very chewy seeds. Often these are discarded and only the flesh used in cooking. In this slow-cooked Iranian dish the seeds have time to soften.

1 lb (450 g) lean lamb, cut into ½ inch (1 cm) cubes
1 level tblsp vegetable oil
1 medium onion, chopped
1 medium aubergine, finely diced
4 oz (100 g) yellow split peas, soaked and drained
4 medium tomatoes, peeled and sliced
flesh and seeds of 1 large pomegranate
½ level tsp ground allspice
½ level tsp ground ginger
2 level tblsp lemon juice
salt and pepper
1 lb (450 g) Basmati rice
1 oz (25 g) butter
2 level tblsp pine nuts

1. Dry-fry the lamb in a non-stick pan for 5 minutes over moderate heat. Stir frequently so that it browns evenly. Lift it out with a draining spoon and set aside.
2. Add the oil and stir-fry the onion and aubergine for 3 minutes.
3. Return the meat to the pan, add the peas, tomatoes, pomegranate, spices and lemon juice and season with salt and pepper. Stir well and cover the pan.
4. Simmer for 1½ hours, stirring occasionally. Add a little water if the sauce becomes too dry.
5. Cook the rice according to the directions on the packet. Toss in butter and stir in the nuts.
6. Make a ring of rice and pile the lamb and pomegranate sauce in the centre.

Sunrise Lamb
Serves 6

2½ lb (1 kg) lean lamb, cut into 1 inch (2.5 cm) cubes
2 medium onions, thinly sliced
2 red peppers, seeded and thinly sliced
3 medium tomatoes, skinned and sliced
3 level tblsp chopped mint
¾ pt (15 fl oz) chicken stock
4 oz (100 g) dried apricots, soaked and drained
salt and pepper

1. In a non-stick pan, dry-fry the meat for 5 minutes, turning it frequently to brown on all sides. Remove with a draining spoon and set aside.
2. Fry the onions and peppers in the fat in the pan for 2 minutes, then add the tomatoes and 2 level tablespoons of the mint. Stir well and simmer for 3 minutes.
3. Return the meat to the pan, add the stock and apricots and bring to the boil.
4. Cover and simmer for 2 hours, stirring occasionally. Season with salt and pepper, and garnish with the reserved mint. Serve with brown rice.

Lamb and Raisin Meatballs
Serves 6

1 lb (450 g) lean lamb, minced
1 small onion, finely chopped
1 egg, lightly beaten
4 level tblsp seedless raisins, finely chopped
2 level tblsp chopped parsley
½ level tsp ground allspice
¼ level tsp ground cinnamon
salt and pepper
½ pt (275 ml) plain low-fat yoghurt
parsley sprigs, to garnish

1. Mix all the ingredients, except the yoghurt and parlsey sprigs, to make a smooth, moist paste — a food processor does it in moments.
2. Flour your hands and form the mixture into small balls, a little larger than walnuts.
3. Arrange them in a shallow pan, pour on the yoghurt and simmer for 15 minutes, shaking the pan often. Garnish with the parsley sprigs. Serve with jacket potatoes or rice.

Coriander Lamb Curry
Serves 4

1 lb (450 g) lean lamb, cut into 1 inch (2.5 cm) cubes
12 spring onions, sliced
2 cloves garlic, crushed
1 inch (2.5 cm) fresh root ginger, chopped
2 level tsp ground coriander
6 level tblsp chopped coriander leaves (or broad-leafed parsley)
2 green chillies, seeded and finely chopped
4 medium tomatoes, skinned and sliced
7 fl oz (200 ml) water
salt
2 mangoes, peeled, stoned and sliced

1. Dry-fry the lamb in a non-stick pan over moderate heat, stirring often, for 4-5 minutes.
2. Remove the meat and stir-fry the onions, garlic and ginger in the pan for 2 minutes. Stir in the ground coriander for 1 minute.
3. Add the chopped coriander, chillies, tomatoes, water and salt and bring to the boil. Cover and simmer for 55 minutes.

4. Stir in all but 4 slices of the mango without breaking them. Simmer for 5 minutes.
5. Garnish with the reserved mango slices. Serve with rice.

Osso Bucco with Gooseberries

Serves 6

2½ lb (1 kg) shank of veal, in 1½ inch (4 cm) slices
2 level tblsp flour
salt and pepper
1 level tblsp crumbled rosemary
1 oz (25 g) butter
1 medium carrot, thinly sliced
1 medium onion, thinly sliced
1 clove garlic, crushed
½ pt (275 ml) dry white wine
½ pt (275 ml) chicken stock
8 oz (225 g) fresh gooseberries
2 level tblsp chopped parsley

1. Toss the veal in the flour seasoned with salt, pepper and rosemary. Brown it on all sides in the butter, remove from the pan and set aside.
2. Fry the carrot, onion and garlic over moderate heat for 3 minutes. Return the veal to the pan, pour on the wine and stock and boil for 15 minutes to reduce the liquid.
3. Cover and simmer for 35 minutes. Add the gooseberries and simmer uncovered for 25-30 minutes until the veal is tender. Adjust the seasoning. Add a pinch of sugar if the sauce is too sharp. Garnish with the parsley. Serve with rice.

Veal Chops with Cranberries

Serves 4

Cranberries are small, round deep red fruits, native to North America and available fresh from October to December, and frozen. They are traditional in a stuffing for the Thanksgiving turkey.

4 veal chops, trimmed of excess fat
1 small onion, finely chopped
1 clove garlic, crushed
¼ pt (150 ml) orange juice
grated rind of ½ orange
salt and pepper
8 oz (225 g) fresh or frozen cranberries
1 level tblsp clear honey
½ oz (15 g) softened butter
1 level tsp flour

1. Dry-fry the chops in a non-stick pan over moderate heat to brown them on both sides. Remove them from the pan and fry the onion and garlic for 2-3 minutes, stirring once or twice.
2. Add the orange juice and rind, season with salt and pepper and return to the boil, cover and simmer for 15 minutes.
3. Add the cranberries and honey. Cover and simmer for a further 5 minutes. Do not allow the berries to break up.
4. Mix butter and flour to a smooth paste.
5. Transfer the chops to a serving dish. Stir the paste into the sauce and stir for 2-3 minutes until it thickens and is glossy. Pour over the chops.

Casserole of Beef with Prunes

Serves 4

2 lb (900 g) lean braising beef, trimmed of excess fat and cut into 1½ inch (4 cm) cubes
2 medium onions, chopped
2 cloves garlic, finely chopped
4 rashers back bacon, rind removed, cut into 1 inch (2.5 cm) squares
2 level tblsp flour
salt and pepper
a pinch of grated nutmeg
¼ level tsp ground allspice
8 oz (225 g) pre-soaked prunes
½ pt (275 ml) red wine
½ pt (275 ml) beef stock
2 level tblsp tomato purée
½ oz (15 g) softened butter
1 level tblsp flour

1. Mix the onions, garlic and bacon and dry-fry in a non-stick pan over moderate heat for 3 minutes, stirring once or twice.
2. Toss the meat cubes in the flour seasoned with salt, pepper, nutmeg and allspice.
3. In a flameproof casserole, make layers of the onion mixture, beef cubes and prunes.
4. Mix together the wine, stock and tomato purée and pour on to the casserole. Bring slowly to the boil and cover.
5. Cook in the oven at 250°F (120°C) Gas ½ for 2 ½ hours, or until the meat is tender.
6. Mix the butter and flour to a paste and, on top of the stove, stir it a little at a time into the sauce. Stir until it thickens and becomes glossy.

Jacket potatoes are a good accompaniment. Boil them for 5-10 minutes first, according to size, then bake them alongside the casserole.

Plantain and Beef Loaf

Serves 8

Choose ripe plantains — they look like large green bananas — which are readily available in West Indian food stores. This recipe come from Honduras.

2 ripe plantains, peeled
1 medium onion, chopped
1 clove garlic, chopped
1 level tblsp vegetable oil
1 red pepper, seeded and chopped
8 oz (225 g) tomatoes, peeled and chopped
2 lb (900 g) beef skirt, minced
2 level tblsp flour
1 large egg, beaten
salt and pepper
¼ level tsp cayenne
thin slices of lime or lemon, to garnish

1. Boil the plantains for 10 minutes. Drain and chop.
2. Fry the onion and garlic in the oil over moderate heat for 3 minutes, stirring once or twice.
3. Combine all the ingredients — for a smooth texture use a food processor. In this case, only roughly chop the vegetables.
4. Press the mixture into a greased 2 pt (1 litre) loaf tin and cover with foil.
5. Place the tin in a roasting pan with 2 inches (5 cm) of water. Bake in the oven at 350° F (180°C), Gas 4 for 1¾ hours. Turn out and garnish with the lime or lemon slices.

* Serve hot, with tomato or barbecue sauce and rice. Or cold — good for left overs — with a fruit sauce and rice salad tossed with sliced peaches.

South American Beef Turnovers

Makes 12-16

1 lb (450 g) wholewheat flour
2 level tsp baking powder
salt
6 oz (175 g) butter
6 oz (175 g) margarine
1 egg yolk, beaten
2 level tblsp plain yoghurt

Filling

1 lb (450 g) minced veal
1 medium onion, finely chopped
1 green pepper, seeded and finely chopped
2 pears, peeled, cored and chopped
2 peaches, peeled, stoned and chopped
4 medium tomatoes, skinned and chopped
¼ pt (150 ml) dry white wine
1 level tblsp tomato purée
salt and pepper
a pinch of cayenne
milk, for brushing

1. To make the pastry, mix the flour, baking powder and salt. Rub in the butter and margarine until the mixture is dry and crumbly. Stir in the egg yolk and yoghurt and form into a dough. Wrap in clingfilm or foil and chill for at least 30 minutes.

2. Dry-fry the veal in a non-stick pan, stirring frequently for 5 minutes over moderate heat. Remove with a draining spoon. Fry the onion and pepper in the fat in the pan for 3 minutes, stirring once or twice.

3. Return the meat to the pan, add the chopped pears, peaches, tomatoes, wine and tomato purée and season with salt, pepper and cayenne. Bring to the boil and simmer for 5 minutes until the excess liquid has been absorbed. Cool the mixture before filling the turnovers.

4. Roll out the dough and cut it into 5 inch (12.5 cm) circles. Dampen the edge of each circle, place filling on one side, fold over and seal the joins. Brush the tops with milk.

5. Place on a baking sheet and bake in the oven at 400°F (200°C), Gas 6 for 15 minutes. Reduce the heat to 350°F (180°C) Gas 4 and bake for a further 25-30 minutes. Serve hot or cold.

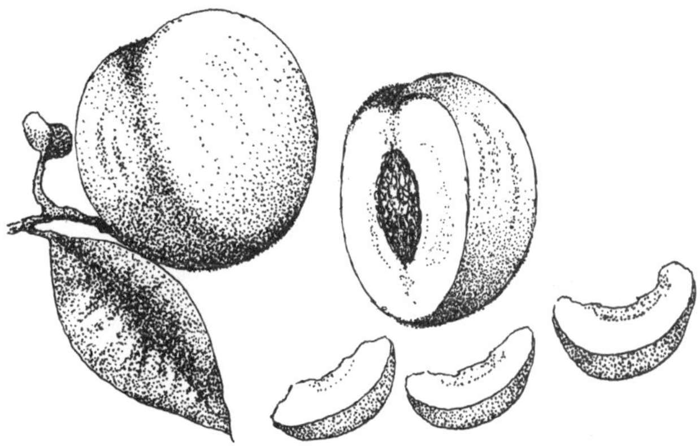

West Indian Beef and Pumpkin Stew

Serves 6-8

2 lb (900 g) topside beef, cut into 1 inch (2.5 cm) cubes
2 medium onions, thinly sliced
1 clove garlic, finely chopped
1 green pepper, seeded and thinly sliced
2 medium tomatoes, skinned and chopped
salt and pepper
1 bay leaf
½ pt (275 ml) red wine
¼ pt (150 ml) beef stock
1 lb (450 g) sweet potatoes, cut into 1 inch (2.5 cm) cubes
1 lb (450 g) pumpkin, cut into 1 inch (2.5 cm) cubes
8 oz (225 g) can tiny sweetcorn cobs (from Oriental grocers), drained
4 peaches, peeled, stoned and quartered

1. Dry-fry the meat in a non-stick pan over moderate heat for 5 minutes, stirring frequently. Remove it with a draining spoon and fry the onions, garlic and pepper for 3 minutes, stirring once or twice.
2. Return the beef to the pan, add the tomatoes, salt, pepper, bay leaf, wine and stock, bring to the boil and simmer for 3 minutes.
3. Cover the pan and simmer for 1½ hours.
4. Add the sweet potatoes and pumpkin, cover and simmer for 10 minutes. Add the sweetcorn and peaches and simmer for a further 10-15 minutes, or until all the vegetables and fruit are tender.

* When fresh pumpkin is not available, use canned pumpkin chunks. Drain, rinse and drain them and add them with the peaches.

Iranian Apples

Serves 4

4 oz (100 g) yellow split peas, soaked and drained
1 medium onion, finely chopped
1 level tblsp vegetable oil
8 oz (225 g) minced beef
½ level tsp ground cinnamon
a pinch of grated nutmeg
4 level tblsp water
2 level tblsp pine nuts
salt and pepper
4 large cooking apples
parsley sprigs, to garnish

1. Cook the split peas in unsalted, boiling water for 35-40 minutes, or until they are tender. Drain them.
2. Fry the onion in the oil over moderate heat for 3 minutes, then add the beef and spices. Stir-fry for 5 minutes, until the meat has browned.
3. Stir in the water, add the cooked peas and nuts. Season with salt and pepper, cover and simmer for 10 minutes.
4. Cut a slice from the top of each apple and take out the cores. Scoop out the flesh (a grapefruit knife is useful) leaving firm walls. With a sharp knife, slit around the circumference of each apple, taking care not to cut right through.
5. Pack the beef mixture into the apples, piling it up into a mound. Place the apples in a baking dish that fits them tightly. Pour on water to come 1 inch (2.5 cm) up the sides.
6. Bake in the oven at 350°F (180°C), Gas 4 for 20 minutes. Garnish with parsley. Serve with tomato sauce and rice.

Six-fruit Pork Casserole

Serves 6

2 lb (900 g) lean pork, cut into 1 inch (2.5 cm) cubes
2 medium onions, thinly sliced
1 small head of celery, thinly sliced
2 large cloves garlic, crushed
2 level tblsp flour
1 level tsp mild curry powder
1 level tsp pepper
salt
1 level tsp crumbled rosemary
1 pt (575 ml) dry cider
6 oz (175 g) dried apricots, soaked and drained
2 oz (50 g) seedless raisins
2 oz (50 g) stoned dates, chopped
2 dessert apples, cored and thinly sliced
grated rind and juice of 1 orange
grated rind and juice of 1 lemon
2 level tblsp walnut halves, to garnish
2 oranges, segmented, to garnish

1. Dry-fry the meat in a non-stick pan, turning it often to brown evenly. Remove with a draining spoon and keep the meat warm.
2. Fry the onions, celery and garlic in the fat in the pan, stirring now and then, for 3 minutes.
3. Mix together the flour, curry powder, pepper, salt and rosemary. Return the meat to the pan, stir, sprinkle on the flour mixture and stir quickly.
4. Pour on the cider and stir until it forms a sauce. Add the fruit, fruit juice and grated rind and stir well.
5. Either transfer to a casserole and cook in the oven at 275°F (140°C), Gas 1 for 2½ hours, or cover the pan and simmer very gently on top of the stove, stirring from time to time.
6. Garnish with the walnuts and orange segments. Serve with rice and a green salad.

Caribbean Ham Loaf

Serves 6-8

½ oz (15 g) butter, melted
2 level tblsp Demerara sugar
¼ level tsp ground cloves
1½ level tsp mustard powder
4 slices pineapple, peeled and cored
6 oz (175 g) wholemeal breadcrumbs
1½ lb (700 g) lean ham, minced
3 oz (75 g) dried apricots, minced or finely chopped
2 eggs, beaten
1 level tsp ground coriander
¼ pt (150 ml) milk
salt and pepper

1. Brush a 2 lb (900 g) loaf tin with the butter. Mix together the sugar, cloves and ½ level teaspoon of the mustard powder and sprinkle on the butter. Halve the pineapple slices and arrange them in the base of the tin.
2. Mix together the breadcrumbs, ham, apricots, eggs, coriander and milk and season well with salt and pepper.
3. Press the mixture into the tin and cover with foil. Place in a roasting pan with 2 inches (5 cm) of water. Bake in the oven at 350°F (180°C), Gas 4 for 1¼ hours. Remove the foil 30 minutes before the end of cooking time.

Serve hot, perhaps with baked tomatoes and courgettes, or cold with rice and pineapple salad.

Liver in Raspberry Sauce

Serves 4

1 lb (450 g) calf's liver, thinly sliced
3 level tblsp flour
salt and pepper
1 level tsp finely crumbled rosemary
1 oz (25 g) butter
1 level tblsp vegetable oil
1 level tsp flour
6 oz fresh or frozen raspberries, liquidized and sieved (reserve a few for garnish)
6 level tblsp chicken stock
2 level tblsp lemon juice
2 level tblsp sweet sherry
mint sprigs, to garnish

1. Toss the liver in the flour seasoned with the salt, pepper and rosemary. Fry the slices in the butter and oil over moderate heat for 1½-2 minutes on each side. Remove the liver and keep it warm.
2. Stir the flour into the pan, then the raspberry purée, stock, lemon juice and sherry. Bring to the boil and simmer for 3-4 minutes until the sauce thickens. Adjust seasoning.
3. Arrange the liver on a dish, pour over the sauce and garnish with the mint and reserved raspberries.

VEGETABLE DISHES

There aren't a great many traditional or classic combinations of vegetables and fruit that spring readily to mind. Perhaps the Northern European hot-pot of shredded red cabbage with apples simmered in beer or wine is the best-known, with a version of the Turkish dish, Imam Bayaldi — aubergines filled with rice and dried fruits — in second place.

That's not good enough! I have found that fruits — dried ones especially — add depth of flavour and extra interest to vegetables cooked and served in today's way, with little or no fat and the minimum of salt. There's nothing like a handful of sultanas or raisins to spark up a dish of steamed potatoes or simmered beans, for example.

When it's flavour you're after, oranges and lemons are well to the fore. Try cooking carrots with the full impact of oranges, and braising celery with a generous amount of lemon juice and a sprinkling of dried apricots for good measure.

Look to fresh and dried fruit, again, to do unusual things to pasta and grains. Avocado makes a green and creamy sauce for spaghetti; dried mulberries combined with rice for a Greek dish of stuffed vine leaves; raisins are naturals in Middle-Eastern pilaffs, and dried peaches, dates and prunes offer an exotic introduction to bulghar.

Sweetened Peas

Serves 4

1 medium onion, finely chopped
½ oz (15 g) butter
1 lb (450 g) shelled peas
6 level tblsp chicken stock
1 level tsp clear honey
salt and pepper
4 oz (100 g) seedless white grapes
2 level tblsp chopped mint

1. Fry the onion in the butter for 2-3 minutes over moderate heat. Add the peas, stock and honey and season with salt and pepper.
2. Cover and simmer for 8 minutes.
3. Add the grapes and simmer for a further 3-4 minutes, until the peas are just tender. Garnish with the chopped mint and serve at once.

This dish is specially good with lamb, and with white fish.

Green Beans almost à la Grecque

Serves 4

1 lb (450 g) small young green beans, topped and tailed
3 dessert apples, cored and thinly sliced

Sauce
¼ pt (150 ml) white wine
¼ pt (150 ml) water
4 level tblsp tomato purée
3 level tblsp vegetable oil
1 medium onion, finely chopped
1 garlic clove, finely chopped
salt and pepper
2 level tblsp sultanas

1. Mix together the sauce ingredients.
2. Put the beans and apples in a pan, pour on the sauce, bring to the boil, cover and simmer over low heat for 40 minutes, stirring occasionally. Scatter with the sultanas to garnish.

Serve hot, to accompany grilled or roast meats, or cold, as an appetizer.

Carrots Glazed with Oranges
Serves 4

2 oranges
1 lb (450 g) carrots, cut into matchstick strips
3 level tblsp chicken stock
1 level tblsp light Muscovado sugar
1 level tblsp chopped parsley

1. Thinly pare the rind of 1 orange, cut it into very thin strips and boil in water for 10 minutes. Drain and pat dry.
2. Cook the carrots over moderate heat in a covered pan with the stock, juice of both oranges and the sugar for 15 minutes, or until the liquid has evaporated and the vegetables are just beginning to brown.

Serve the carrots sprinkled with the orange strips and ringed with parsley for colour contrast.

Golden Celery
Serves 4

2 heads celery
2 lemons
6 level tblsp chicken stock
4 oz (100 g) dried apricots, soaked, drained and quartered
2 level tblsp blanched almonds, toasted

1. Discard any discoloured outside leaves. Slice the celery hearts lengthways into 3. Use the outer leaves and tops for soup.
2. Cook the celery over moderate heat in a covered, shallow pan with the juice of both lemons and the grated rind of 1, the stock and the apricots for 15-20 minutes.
3. Garnish with the toasted almonds just before serving.

Red Cabbage
Serves 4

¼ pt (150 ml) water
¼ pt (150 ml) red wine
2 level tblsp red wine vinegar
1 small red cabbage, cored and shredded
1 medium cooking apple, peeled, cored and diced
1 medium onion, sliced
salt and pepper
1 level tblsp redcurrant jelly

1. Heat the water, wine and vinegar to just below boiling point.
2. Add the cabbage, apple and onion and season with salt and pepper.
3. Cover and simmer for 1 hour, stirring occasionally. Stir in the redcurrant jelly and add more seasoning if needed. Serve hot.

This dish is traditionally served with game, beef, pork and ham.

Cranberried Turnips

Serves 4

1 lb (450 g) small white turnips, diced
4 oz (100 g) frozen cranberries
2 level tblsp clear honey
1 level tblsp orange juice

1. Steam the turnips over fast-boiling water for 15-20 minutes, until they are just tender.

2. Simmer the cranberries with the honey and orange juice for 3-4 minutes. Do not let the fruit collapse.

3. Toss the turnips in the berries to brighten and glaze them.

Aubergine Boats

Serves 4

4 small aubergines
1 medium onion, chopped
1 small red pepper, seeded and chopped
1 small green pepper, seeded and chopped
4 level tblsp sultanas
4 dried apple rings, thinly sliced
2 dried pears, soaked, drained and chopped
8 level tblsp chicken stock
salt and pepper
2 level tblsp chopped hazelnuts
1 level tblsp chopped parsley
1 level tblsp chopped mint
12 oz (350 g) low-fat cottage cheese

1. Halve the aubergines lengthways, scoop out the flesh without breaking the skins, and chop it finely.

2. Simmer the aubergine flesh, chopped onion, peppers and dried fruits in the stock for 10 minutes, until the liquid has been absorbed but the mixture is still moist.

3. Season the mixture with salt and pepper, stir in the nuts and herbs and pile into the aubergine shells. Spread the cottage cheese on top.

4. Grill for 5 minutes, until the cheese topping is brown and bubbling. Serve with grilled tomatoes, and rice.

Vegetable Curry

Serves 4

2 medium potatoes, peeled and diced
1 small cauliflower, cut into florets
2 medium leeks, sliced
1 medium onion, chopped
2 level tblsp vegetable oil
½ level tsp ground turmeric
½ level tsp ground cumin
½ level tsp ground black pepper
¼ level tsp coriander seed
8 oz (225 g) canned tomatoes
¾ pint (425 ml) water
2 pears, peeled, cored and diced
1 cooking apple, peeled, cored and diced
4 level tblsp sultanas
salt
2 level tsp garam masala
plain low-fat yoghurt, to serve

1. Steam the potatoes, cauliflower and leeks until they are barely tender.

2. Fry the onion in the oil over moderate heat for 2 minutes. Stir in the turmeric, cumin, pepper and coriander and cook for 1 minute, stirring all the time.

3. Add the canned tomatoes and water, bring to the boil, cover and simmer for 20 minutes.

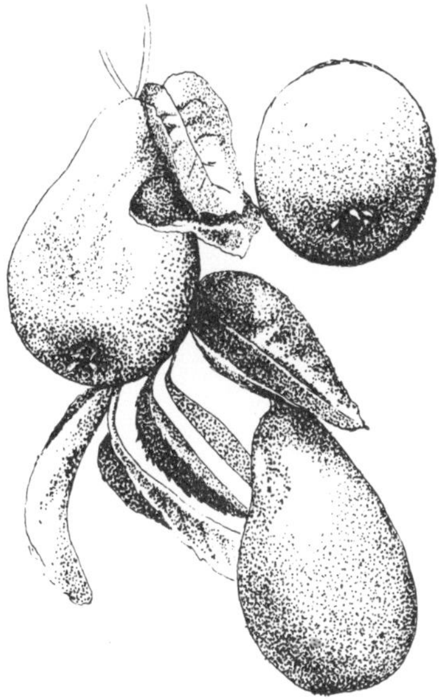

4. Add the steamed vegetables, the pears, apple and sultanas and stir in the salt and garam masala. Simmer for 5-10 minutes, until the fruit is tender. Serve topped with yoghurt.

Brown rice is the natural accompaniment, with fruit chutney and grilled or fried poppadoms.

Avocado Pilaff

Serves 4

1 medium onion, finely chopped
1 level tblsp vegetable oil
8 oz (225 g) brown short-grain rice
¾ pt (425 ml) chicken stock
¼ pt (150 ml) dry cider
salt and pepper
4 oz (100 g) button mushrooms, sliced
1 clove garlic, crushed
4 large tomatoes, skinned, seeded and chopped
½ oz (15 g) butter
1 level tblsp chopped parsley
1 avocado, peeled, stoned and diced
4 tblsp blanched almonds

1. Fry the onion in the oil over moderate heat for 3 minutes, stirring once or twice. Stir in the rice, pour on the stock and cider, season with salt and pepper and bring to the boil.
2. Cover and simmer for 45 minutes, stirring once or twice.
3. While the rice is cooking fry the mushrooms, garlic and tomatoes in the butter over low heat for 5 minutes, stirring often.
4. Stir in the parsley and avocado and gently heat through.
5. Make a ring of rice, pile the avocado mixture into the centre and scatter with the almonds.

This substantial rice dish is good with a tomato and herb salad and crisp, cool salad greens.

Stuffed Vine Leaves
Serves 6

1 lb (450 g) jar or can of vine leaves
2 level tblsp vegetable oil
1 small onion, finely chopped
1 clove garlic, crushed
2 dessert apples, peeled, cored and chopped
6 oz (150 g) cooked brown rice
6 level tblsp orange juice
2 level tblsp chopped mint
2 level tblsp pine nuts, or slivered almonds
2 oz (50 g) dried mulberries
4 oz (100 g) dried apricots, soaked, drained and chopped
salt and pepper

Sauce
¼ pt (150 ml) chicken stock
½ pt (275 ml) plain low-fat yoghurt
1 level tblsp lemon juice

1. Drain the vine leaves, separate each roll carefully and spread them out in a large bowl. Pour on boiling water to cover and leave for 20 minutes. Drain the leaves and pat them dry.
2. Heat the oil and fry the onion, garlic and apple over moderate heat for 3-4 minutes, stirring frequently.
3. Stir in the rice, orange juice, mint, nuts and dried fruit. Season with salt and pepper.
4. Place the leaves flat with the stalk end towards you. Spoon a little filling in the centre of each. Roll up from the bottom to enclose the filling and fold over the sides to make tight, neat parcels.
5. Arrange the stuffed leaves, joined sides down, in a large, shallow baking dish.
6. Mix the stock, yoghurt and lemon juice, season with salt and pepper and pour over the leaves.
7. Cover the dish with foil and bake in the oven at 325°F (170°C), Gas 3 for 45 minutes.

Serve hot, with green salad, or cold, as an appetizer.

Fruit and Nut Pilaff
Serves 4

2 level tblsp vegetable oil
8 oz (225 g) brown short-grain rice
1 pt (575 ml) chicken stock, boiling
1 medium onion, sliced
1 clove garlic, crushed
2 stalks celery, thinly sliced
1 red pepper, seeded and chopped
1 green pepper, seeded and chopped
4 oz (100 g) button mushrooms, quartered
2 oz cashews, chopped
2 oz (50 g) seedless raisins
2 oz (50 g) sultanas
salt and pepper
4 oz (100 g) black grapes, skinned and seeded

1. Fry the rice in 1 tablespoon of the oil for 2-3 minutes over moderate heat, stirring. Pour on the boiling stock, stir, cover and simmer for 45 minutes.
2. Fry the onion, garlic, celery, chopped pepper and mushrooms in the remaining oil for 3 minutes, stirring once or twice.
3. Stir this vegetable mixture into the rice with the nuts, dried fruit and salt and pepper and heat through over low heat. Just before serving, stir in the black grapes. Serve with green salad.

Bulghar Luncheon
Serves 4-6

8 oz (225 g) bulghar (cracked wheat)
½ pt (275 ml) chicken stock, boiling
2 level tblsp vegetable oil
1 large onion, finely chopped
2 large leeks, thinly sliced
1 large carrot, diced
1 red pepper, seeded and chopped
6 level tblsp boiling water
2 large tomatoes, skinned and chopped
2 oz (50 g) seedless raisins
4 dried peach halves, soaked, drained and chopped
8 pre-soaked prunes, halved and pitted
2 oz (50 g) stoned dates, chopped
salt and pepper
1 level tblsp chopped parsley
2 oz (50 g) Cheddar cheese, grated

1. Soak the bulghar for 10 minutes in the boiling stock.

2. Heat the oil and fry the onion, leeks, carrot and pepper in a non-stick pan over moderate heat for 5 minutes, stirring often. Add the boiling water, cover and simmer for 15 minutes, stirring once or twice.

3. Mix together the bulghar and vegetables, stir in the tomatoes and dried fruit and heat gently, stirring all the time. Season well with salt and pepper and stir in the parsley. Sprinkle with the grated cheese.

Spaghetti with Avocado Sauce
Serves 4

1 lb (450 g) wholewheat spaghetti
salt
½ small cauliflower, cut into florets
2 medium carrots, thinly sliced
2 medium leeks, sliced
8 oz (225 g) tomatoes, skinned and chopped
pepper
2 small avocados, peeled, stoned and thinly sliced
½ pt (275 ml) plain low-fat yoghurt
4 level tblsp pumpkin seeds

1. Cook the spaghetti in plenty of boiling, salted water for 10-12 minutes, or until it is just tender. Drain, refresh it in hot water and drain thoroughly. Keep the pasta warm.

2. Steam the cauliflower, carrots and leeks until they are just tender.

3. Toss the tomatoes with the hot spaghetti.

4. Toss the cooked vegetables with the avocado and yoghurt and heat gently.

5. Pour the sauce over the spaghetti and scatter with the pumpkin seeds.

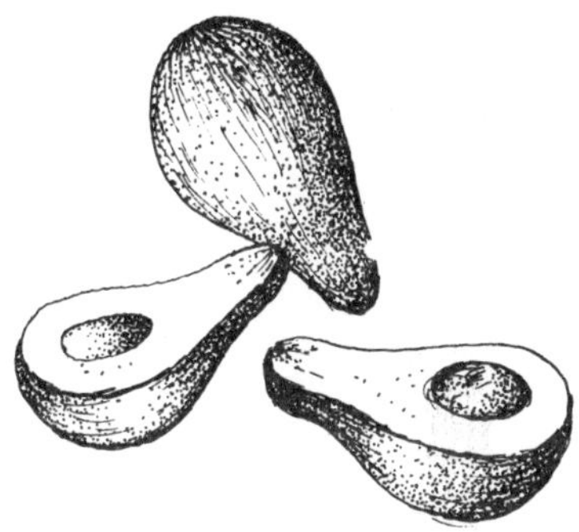

Coconut Rice

Serves 4

8 oz (225 g) desiccated coconut
1¼ pt (724 ml) boiling water
8 oz (225 g) seedless raisins
8 oz (225 g) brown short-grain rice
1 level tblsp light Muscovado sugar
salt
½ oz (15 g) butter

1. Soak the coconut in the boiling water for 20 minutes, then strain through a fine colander. Press the coconut firmly with the back of a spoon to extract all the liquid.

2. Soak the raisins in the coconut 'milk' for 30 minutes. Strain, reserving the raisins. Measure the liquid and make it up to 1 pint (575 ml) if necessary with water.

3. Put the raisins, coconut liquid, rice, sugar and salt into a pan, stir well and bring to the boil. Cover and simmer very gently for 45 minutes, stirring once or twice.

4. Stir in the butter. Serve at once.

This sweet-rice dish from South America is a good accompaniment to poultry and pork.

Banana and Date Bread (page 61)

Overleaf: left: Caribbean Cup (page 85); centre: Banana Flip (page 86); right: Blackcurrant Yoghurt (page 86)

SAVOURY SALADS

Light and refreshing, crisp and crunchy, wholesome and healthy, savoury salads can be served at all times and everywhere. As a first course to excite the imagination without dulling the appetite; as a side dish to accompany more substantial fare; as a course in their own right, at a formal meal or a picnic; and as a 'chaser' after richer foods: savoury salads are a menu planner's best friend.

Dried and fresh fruits play their part to the full, adding nutrients, colour, flavour, texture and innumerable opportunities to ring the changes. Try using shiny-black prunes in place of olives in a Greek-style cheese salad — and in salad Niçoise too; toss chopped dates or dried vine fruits with vegetables that can be a scrap bitter, such as cauliflower and chicory, and with bland ingredients like pasta and rice. Toss fresh fruits — blackberries, apples, pears, grapefruit, lychees, kiwi fruit, pineapple —with conventional salad ingredients and salads will never be conventional again.

Blackberry and Apple Salad

Serves 4

8 oz (225 g) cottage cheese
2 level tblsp sunflower seeds
3 dessert apples, cored and thinly sliced
2 level tblsp lemon juice
8 oz (225 g) blackberries
4 level tblsp cashews
1 small endive, to serve

1. Line a serving plate with the endive, reserving a few of the frilliest leaves to garnish.
2. Mix the cheese and sunflower seeds and pile into the centre of the leaves.
3. Toss the apple slices in lemon juice and arrange in a ring around the cheese. Arrange rings of blackberries on each side of the apples.
4. Sprinkle on the cashew nuts and arrange the endive sprigs to garnish.

Fennel and Grape Salad

Serves 4

2 bulbs fennel, thinly sliced
2 spring onions, thinly sliced
2 oranges, segmented
4 oz (100 g) black grapes, seeded
½ bunch watercress sprigs

Dressing
2 level tblsp vegetable oil
1 level tblsp orange juice
1 level tblsp red wine vinegar
salt and pepper
½ level tsp fennel seeds, lightly crushed

1. Mix together the dressing ingredients. Cover and set aside for at least 30 minutes, for the flavours to blend.
2. Toss together the fennel, onions, orange segments and grapes.
3. Strain the dressing to remove the seeds. Pour over the salad and toss to coat it evenly. Garnish the dish with the watercress sprigs.

French Bean and Orange Salad

Serves 4

1 lb (450 g) green beans, topped and tailed
salt
3 oranges, skinned, seeded and very thinly sliced into rings
4 level tblsp seedless raisins
2 large onions, sliced into rings
1 box salad cress, to garnish

Dressing
1 level tblsp vegetable oil
1 level tsp coriander seeds, lightly crushed
½ level tsp ground coriander
2 level tblsp orange juice
2 level tblsp chopped coriander leaves, or flat-leafed parsley

1. Mix the dressing.
2. Cook the beans in boiling, salted water until they are just tender. Drain, plunge into cold water, drain and dry thoroughly on crumpled kitchen paper.
3. Arrange the orange slices in overlapping rings on a plate and scatter with the raisins.
4. Gather the beans into bunches of about 6 or 7 and push them through an onion ring to hold them neatly — like a napkin ring. Scatter the remaining onion rings over the oranges.
5. Arrange the 'bean sticks' on the oranges and garnish with tiny bunches of salad cress.
6. Sprinkle the dressing over the salad just before serving.

Orange and Mushroom Salad
Serves 4

½ small endive, to serve
3 oranges, segmented
1 bunch watercress sprigs
4 oz (100 g) button mushrooms, thinly sliced

Dressing
4 level tblsp vegetable oil
2 level tblsp red wine vinegar
1 level tblsp orange juice
salt and pepper
1 clove garlic, crushed
1 level tblsp snipped chives
1 level tblsp chopped black olives

1. Mix together all the dressing ingredients except the olives.
2. Line a dish with the endive leaves. Arrange a ring of orange sements then a ring of watercress sprigs. Just before serving, drizzle on about one-third of the dressing.
3. Stir the olives into the remaining dressing and toss in the mushrooms. Pile into the centre of the dish.

Oriental Salad
Serves 4

Lychees, a tree fruit originating in China, are now also grown in India and South Africa. They are almost round, and about the size of cooking plums. The brown skin is rough and knobbly but the fruit surrounding the stone is colourless, translucent, juicy and sweet.

2 heads chicory
½ bunch watercress
12 radishes, thinly sliced
6 oz (175 g) fresh bean sprouts, washed and drained
4 lychees, peeled, stoned and sliced

Dressing
2 level tblsp vegetable oil
1 level tsp soy sauce
2 level tblsp orange juice
1 level tblsp clear honey

1. Mix the dressing to dissolve the honey.
2. Toss together all the salad ingredients.
3. Just before serving, toss the salad in the dressing.

Pantry Salad
Serves 4

3 oz (75 g) dried red kidney beans, soaked and drained
3 oz (75 g) dried flageolets, soaked and drained
4 oz (100g) dried apricots, quartered
2 oz (50 g) seedless raisins
1 small onion, thinly sliced into rings
1 orange, segmented
torn endive leaves, to serve.

Dressing
3 level tblsp vegetable oil
1 level tblsp red wine vinegar
1 level tblsp orange juice
1 level tsp ginger syrup
salt and pepper

1. Bring the kidney beans and flageolets to the boil in separate pans of unsalted water and boil vigorously for 10 minutes. Cover and boil for a further 50 minutes, or until the beans are tender. Drain. Or use left-over beans from another dish, or canned beans, drained and rinsed.

2. Meanwhile, mix together the ingredients for the dressing. Toss in the hot beans and leave them to cool.

3. Stir in the dried fruits.

4. Line a dish with the endive and spoon on the salad. Garnish with the onion rings and orange segments.

Fruit Basket Cole Slaw
Serves 4

½ small white cabbage, shredded
2 dessert apples, cored and chopped
2 oranges, segmented
3 oz (75 g) seedless raisins
3 slices pineapple, peeled, cored and diced
4 oz (100 g) peanuts
4 level tblsp sesame seeds

Dressing
¼ pt (150 ml) plain low-fat yoghurt
1 slice pineapple, finely chopped
1 level tblsp cider vinegar
pepper

1. Mix the dressing ingredients.

2. Toss together the cabbage, fruit and nuts and stir in the dressing. Sprinkle the sesame seeds on top.

High-Fibre Salad
Serves 4

4 oz (100 g) dried chickpeas, soaked and drained
1 small cauliflower
salt
4 spring onions, chopped
2 oz (50 g) sultanas
3 oz (75 g) chopped dates
salad leaves, to serve
watercress sprigs, to garnish

Dressing
¼ pt (150 ml) plain low-fat yoghurt
2 level tblsp pineapple juice
pepper

1. Cook the chickpeas in boiling, unsalted water for 2 hours, or until they are tender. Drain and cool. Or use left-over cooked dried peas or canned ones, rinsed and drained.

2. Trim the stalk from the cauliflower. Cook the vegetable in boiling, salted water until it is barely tender. Plunge into cold water, then drain and dry thoroughly.

3. Toss together the chickpeas, onions, sultanas and dates.
4. Mix together the yoghurt and pineapple juice and season with pepper. Stir the dressing into the chickpea salad and mix well.
5. Line a plate with salad leaves. Place the cauliflower in the centre and cut it almost through into 8 wedges, so that it opens out. Pile the salad in the centre. Garnish with watercress sprigs.

Mango and Avocado Salad

Serves 4

2 mangoes, peeled, stoned and thinly sliced
2 avocados, peeled, stoned and thinly sliced
1 small endive, to serve
lime or lemon slices, to garnish

Dressing
1 level tsp Worcestershire sauce
1 level tsp red wine vinegar
1 egg
juice and grated rind of ½ lime or 1 small lemon
salt

1. Beat the dressing ingredients.
2. Line a serving dish with the endive.
3. Toss the mango and avocado slices in the dressing. Arrange them on the salad leaves, garnish with the lime or lemon slices.

Curried Rice Salad

Serves 6

4 oz (100 g) brown long-grain rice
salt
2 red peppers, grilled, skinned, seeded and thinly sliced (see page 54)
2 green peppers, grilled, skinned, seeded and thinly sliced
4 medium tomatoes, thinly sliced
4 oz (100 g) sultanas
4 oz (100 g) chopped dates
4 oz (100 g) seedless grapes, or white grapes, skinned and seeded
2 oz (50 g) walnuts, roughly chopped
2 oz (50 g) hazelnuts

Dressing
1 level tsp mild curry powder
1 level tsp vegetable oil
1 level tsp lemon juice
pepper
½ pt (275 ml) plain low-fat yoghurt

1. Cook the rice in plenty of boiling, salted water for 40 minutes. Drain, refresh in cold water and drain again.
2. Toss together the rice, peppers, tomatoes, fruit and nuts. Cover and chill for at least 1 hour.
3. Mix the curry powder into a paste with the oil. Stir in the lemon juice and beat the mixture into the yoghurt.
4. Toss the salad in the dressing and serve chilled. This colourful salad makes a good 'basic' part of a cold buffet.

It is a tasty accompaniment to cold meats.

Tropical Date Salad
Serves 4

2 small ugli fruit, segmented
8 oz (225 g) fresh dates
2 small lettuce hearts
½ bunch watercress sprigs

Dressing
2 level tblsp vegetable oil
1 piece preserved ginger, finely chopped
1 level tsp ginger syrup
1 level tblsp lemon juice
salt and pepper

1. Mix the dressing.

2. Toss together the fruit, lettuce leaves and watercress sprigs.

3. Just before serving, pour the dressing over the salad and toss well until each leaf glistens.

Grilled Pepper Salad
Serves 4

2 red peppers
2 green peppers
3 level tblsp vegetable oil
1 level tblsp orange juice
2 cloves garlic, finely chopped
2 level tblsp chopped parsley
salt and pepper
2 dessert pears, peeled, cored and thinly sliced
1 level tblsp lemon juice
2 level tblsp black olives

1. Grill the peppers under moderate heat turning them often, until the skins are black. Hold each pepper on a fork or skewer under cold water. Peel off the skins. Cut the peppers, remove the seeds and pith and cut the flesh into strips.

2. Bring the oil and orange juice to the boil, pour over the peppers and leave to cool. Stir in the garlic and parsley and season with salt and pepper.

3. Toss the pears in lemon juice then toss them with the pepper. Garnish with the olives.

Iceberg Platter
Serves 6

8 oz (225 g) green tagliatelle
salt
2 level tblsp vegetable oil
1 level tblsp lemon juice
pepper
8 oz (225 g) mange-tout peas, topped and tailed
1 green dessert apple, cored and very thinly sliced
4 oz (100 g) seedless grapes, or white grapes, skinned and seeded
1 kiwi fruit, skinned and thinly sliced to garnish
1 iceberg lettuce, cut in wedges, to serve

1. Cook the tagliatelle in boiling, salted water until just tender, about 10 minutes. Drain.

2. Mix together the oil and lemon juice and season with salt and pepper. Toss the hot pasta in the dressing and leave to cool.

3. Cook the mange-tout peas in boiling, salted water for 5-6 minutes, or until they are just tender. Drain, refresh in cold water, drain and dry thoroughly on crumpled kitchen paper.

4. Toss together the tagliatelle, peas, apple and grapes. Garnish with a pattern of kiwi fruit slices. Serve with wedges of iceberg lettuce.

Pasta Salad
Serves 4

4 oz (100 g) wholewheat pasta shells
salt
2 dessert apples, cored and thinly sliced
1 level tblsp lemon juice
2 small grapefruit, segmented
3 level tblsp seedless raisins
1 level tblsp vegetable oil
1 level tblsp red wine vinegar
3 level tblsp plain low-fat yoghurt
pepper
spinach or other salad leaves, to serve
2 level tblsp walnut halves

1. Cook the pasta shells in boiling, salted water for 10-12 minutes, until they are just tender. Drain, plunge into cold water, drain and cool. Toss on crumpled kitchen paper to dry thoroughly.

2. Toss the apple slices in the lemon juice, then toss with the pasta, grapefruit and raisins.

3. Mix together the oil, vinegar and yoghurt and season with salt and pepper.

4. Toss the salad in the dressing. Serve on the salad leaves and garnish with the walnuts.

Broad Bean and Pear Salad
Serves 4

1 lb (450 g) shelled broad beans, fresh or frozen
salt
4 oz (100 g) thickly sliced ham, cut into squares
2 dessert pears, peeled, cored and thinly sliced
1 level tblsp lemon juice
raddichio leaves, to serve

Dressing
2 level tblsp vegetable oil
1 level tblsp lemon juice
1 level tblsp clear honey
1 level tblsp chopped mint
2 spring onions, thinly sliced
salt and pepper

1. Mix the dressing.

2. Cook the beans in boiling, salted water until they are just tender. Plunge them into cold water, drain again and toss on crumpled kitchen paper to dry.

3. Mix together the beans and ham and toss them in the dressing.

4. Toss the pear slices in lemon juice.

5. Line a dish with raddichio leaves (or use endive, or corn salad). Pile the bean and ham salad in the centre with the pear slices in a ring around it.

Greek Cheese Salad
Serves 4

1 small cucumber, diced
2 green peppers, seeded and sliced into rings
12 oz (350 g) tomatoes, quartered
3 spring onions, sliced
4 oz (100 g) pre-soaked prunes, halved and stoned
4 oz (100 g) Feta cheese, thinly sliced (or use Wensleydale)

Dressing
4 level tblsp vegetable oil
2 cloves garlic, crushed
2 level tblsp lemon juice
pepper

1. Mix the dressing.
2. Make layers of the salad ingredients in the order given — a glass bowl shows them to best effect.
3. Pour over the dressing just before serving.

This salad is especially good as a side dish with grilled lamb.

Herring Salad

Serves 4

4 fresh herrings, skinned and filleted
1 level tsp pickling spice
4 spring onions, sliced
¼ pt (150 ml) cider vinegar
1 lb (450 g) cherries, stoned
1 level tsp French mustard
¼ pt (150 ml) plain low-fat yoghurt
¼ pt (150 ml) soured cream
pepper
a few raddichio (red chicory) leaves to serve, if available

1. Put the herring fillets, pickling spice, onions and vinegar into a shallow baking dish. Cover with foil and bake in the oven at 350°F (180°C), Gas 4 for 25-30 minutes. Cool.
2. Lift out the herring fillets and discard the liquor and spices. Cool, then add the cherries.
3. Mix together the mustard, yoghurt and soured cream and season well with pepper. Pour over the herrings and cherries and toss to blend well.
4. Line a plate with raddichio or other leaves and spoon on the salad.

Serve with rye bread and green salads.

BAKING

In the context of health foods, baking turns back the clock, bypassing the Industrial Revolution which made refined — I prefer to call them incomplete — flour and sugar so readily available.

By choosing the natural ingredients and using wholemeal flour in bread, scones and pastry you benefit from all the nutrients in the germ, and the dietary fibre in the bran, both of which are milled out in the refined product.

And by using fresh or dried fruits in baked goods, you add sweetness in its original form. Where sugar *is* needed, choose the natural ingredients again, the raw cane sugars, Demerara, light and dark Muscovado and the black sticky molasses sugar, which retain important minerals and trace elements. Not only that, because of the much richer and fuller flavour of raw sugars, smaller quantities are needed.

Fresh fruits keep bread and scones appetisingly moist — try banana and date bread, pear and walnut loaf and spicy apple scones — whilst dried fruits contribute a more concentrated flavour — pear teabread tastes *more* of pears — and obviate the need for sweetened spreads. Cottage cheese to my mind makes the perfect spread for fruit loaves of all kinds.

Apple Griddle Scones

Makes 16 scones

3 oz (75 g) wholewheat flour
1 level tsp cream of tartar
½ level tsp bicarbonate of soda
¼ level tsp salt
1 oz (25 g) caster sugar
½ level tsp ground ginger
1 egg
2 level tblsp vegetable oil
¼ pt (150 ml) milk
2 dessert apples, peeled, cored and finely chopped

1. Sift the dry ingredients and beat in the egg, oil and milk. Beat well, cover and set aside for 15 minutes.
2. Stir in the chopped apple.
3. Drop dessertspoonfuls of the batter on to a heated non-stick base (griddle or frying pan). Cook for 1 minute or until the top bubbles, flip over and cook the underside for 1-2 minutes.
4. Wrap the scones in a folded cloth to keep them warm while you cook the remainder. Serve warm, if possible.

Apple and Cinnamon Scones

Makes 10 scones

8 oz (225 g) wholewheat self-raising flour
½ level tsp salt
1 level tsp ground cinnamon
2 oz (50 g) hard margarine
12 oz (350 g) apple purée
¼ pt (150 ml) milk
2 level tblsp Demerara sugar
5 oz (125 g) cottage cheese, sieved

1. Sift together the flour, salt and cinnamon and rub in the margarine. Beat in one-third of the apple purée and the milk. Mix to form a stiff dough.
2. Roll out the dough on a lightly floured board and cut into 2 inch (5 cm) rounds. Brush the tops with milk, sprinkle with the Demerara sugar and place the scones on a baking sheet.
3. Bake in the oven at 450°F (230°C), Gas 8 for 10 minutes. Cool slightly on a wire rack.
4. Serve the scones, warm if possible, halved and split. Sandwich them with the remaining apple purée beaten together with the cottage cheese.

Orange Scones

Makes one 8 inch (20 cm) scone

8 oz (225 g) wholewheat self-raising flour
grated rind and juice of 1 orange
1 oz (25 g) light Muscovado sugar
2 oz (50 g) hard margarine
1 egg, lightly beaten
2 oz (50 g) sultanas
2 level tblsp Demerara sugar, for topping

1. Mix together the flour, orange rind and sugar and rub in the margarine. Stir in the egg and orange juice and then the sultanas.

2. Mix to a soft dough and knead in the bowl until it is smooth.

3. Press the dough into a greased 8 inch (20 cm) round cake tin and level the top. Sprinkle on the sugar.

4. Bake in the oven at 425°F (225°C), Gas 7 for 15 minutes. Cool slightly on a wire rack. The scone is best served warm.

Prune Layer Teabread

Makes one 2 lb (900 g) loaf

10 oz (275 g) wholewheat self-raising flour
salt
½ level tsp ground allspice
a pinch of grated nutmeg
3 oz (75 g) hard margarine
2 oz (50 g) light Muscovado sugar
1 oz (25 g) dried prune flakes
1 egg
3½ fl oz (100 ml) milk
2 oz (50 g) sultanas
3 oz (75 g) pre-soaked prunes, pitted and chopped
milk, for brushing

1. Sift together the flour, salt and spices and rub in the margarine to make crumbs. Stir in the sugar and prune flakes.

2. Lightly beat the egg and milk and beat into the dry ingredients to form a dough.

3. Place half the dough in a greased 2 lb (900 g) loaf tin, level the top and cover with the sultanas and chopped prunes. Cover with the remaining dough, level the top and brush with milk.

4. Bake in the oven at 375°F (190°C), Gas 5 for 50 minutes.

5. Partly cool in the tin. Turn the loaf out on to a wire rack to cool. When completely cold wrap in foil and store for 2-3 days before serving.

Apricot Scone Ring

Makes one 9 inch (23 cm) round

8 oz (225 g) wholemeal flour
1 level tsp bicarbonate of soda
½ level tsp salt
1 level tsp ground cinnamon
a pinch of grated nutmeg
2 oz (50 g) hard margarine
5 oz (125 g) dried apricots, chopped
¼ pt (150 ml) plain low-fat yoghurt
milk, for brushing
2 level tblsp bulghar, for topping

1. Sift together the flour, soda, salt and spices and rub in the margarine. Stir in the apricots and beat in the yoghurt.
2. Mix to form a smooth dough, then knead lightly on a floured board. Shape into a 9 inch (23 cm) round, place on a baking sheet and mark into 8 slices. Brush the top with milk and sprinkle with the cracked wheat.
3. Bake in the oven at 425°F (220°C), Gas 7 for 25 minutes. Cool on a wire rack. It's best eaten on the same day.

Mulberry Cheesebread

Makes one 2 lb (900 g) loaf

8 oz (225 g) cottage cheese, sieved
3 oz (75 g) light Muscovado sugar
2 eggs, lightly beaten
grated rind of 1 orange
3 oz (75 g) ground almonds
5 oz (125 g) wholemeal flour
2 oz (50 g) chopped hazelnuts
3 oz (75 g) dried mulberries

1. Beat the cottage cheese and sugar, then beat in the eggs and orange rind. Stir in the almonds and fold in the flour. Stir in the hazelnuts and mulberries.
2. Turn the mixture into a greased 2 lb (900 g) loaf tin and level the top.
3. Bake in the oven at 350°F (180°C), Gas 4 for 1 hour 10 minutes.
4. Partly cool in the tin, then turn out on to a wire rack.

The cheesebread is very good sliced and eaten with fresh fruit such as apples or peaches.

Date and Ginger Bread

Makes one 1 lb (450 g) loaf

7 oz (200 g) wholewheat flour
1 level tsp baking powder
1 level tsp bicarbonate of soda
1 level tsp ground ginger
2 oz (50 g) hard margarine
2 oz (50 g) light Muscovado sugar
3 oz (75 g) dried, stoned dates, chopped
1 oz (25 g) crystallized ginger, chopped
9 level tblsp milk

1. Sift together the flour, baking powder, soda and ground ginger and rub in the margarine. Stir in the sugar, dates and chopped ginger and mix to a soft dough with the milk.
2. Turn the mixture into a greased 1 lb (450 g) loaf tin and level the top.
3. Bake in the oven at 350°F (180°C), Gas 4 for 1 hour.
4. Partly cool in the tin, then turn on to a wire rack. When completely cold, wrap in foil and store for 1-2 days before serving.

Banana and Date Bread

Makes one 2 lb (900 g) loaf

8 oz (225 g) wholewheat self-raising flour
1 level tsp baking powder
a pinch of bicarbonate of soda
1 level tsp ground cinnamon
3 oz (75 g) light Muscovado sugar
3 oz (75 g) soft margarine
3 medium bananas, mashed
2 eggs
4 oz (100 g) dried dates, chopped

1. Sift together the flour, baking powder, soda and spice and stir in the sugar. Beat in the margarine, bananas and eggs and stir in the chopped dates. Beat until the mixture is smooth.

2. Turn into a greased 2 lb (900 g) loaf tin and level the top.

3. Bake in the oven at 350°F (180°C), Gas 4 for 1 hour 10 minutes. Partly cool in the tin, then turn on to a wire rack to cool. When completely cold, wrap in foil and store for 1-2 days.

Pear Teabread

Makes one 1 lb (450 g) loaf

¼ pt (150 ml) milk
2 level tblsp clear honey
1 egg
9 oz (250 g) wholewheat self-raising flour
salt
1 oz (25 g) margarine
2 oz (50 g) light Muscovado sugar
4 oz (100 g) dried pears, finely chopped
1 level tsp grated lemon rind
2 oz (50 g) chopped walnuts

1. Warm the milk with the honey. Cool and beat in the egg.

2. Rub the flour, salt and fat to make crumbs. Stir in the sugar, pears, lemon rind and walnuts.

3. Beat the egg mixture into the dry ingredients and pour the batter into a greased 1 lb (450 g) loaf tin. Leave to stand for 15 minutes.

4. Bake in the oven at 350°F (180°C), Gas 4 for 50 minutes. Serve warm or cold.

Cottage cheese sieved and beaten with a little honey makes a delicious spread.

Malt Loaf

Makes one 2 lb (900 g) loaf

9 level tblsp malt extract
2 level tblsp dark Muscovado sugar
7 fl oz (200 ml) milk
12 oz (350 g) wholewheat self-raising flour
salt
8 oz (225 g) currants
2 oz (50 g) chopped walnuts
2 eggs, lightly beaten

1. Gently heat the malt extract, sugar and milk, stirring until the mixture has melted. Cool.
2. Sift together the flour and salt and stir in the fruit and nuts.
3. Pour the malt mixture on to the dry ingredients, beat in the eggs and beat well.
4. Turn into a greased 2 lb (900 g) loaf tin. Bake in the oven at 300°F (150°C), Gas 2 for 1½ hours.
5. Partly cool in the tin, then turn on to a wire rack to cool. When completely cold, wrap in foil and store for 2-3 days, before serving.

Spiced Pumpkin Bread

Makes one 9 inch (23 cm) round

8 oz (225 g) pumpkin purée
1 oz (25 g) soft margarine
1 level tsp sugar
1 level tblsp warm water
1 egg, beaten
½ oz (15 g) dried yeast
8 oz (225 g) wholewheat flour
2 level tsp salt
3 oz (75 g) sultanas
½ level tsp cinnamon
½ level tsp ground ginger
a pinch of grated nutmeg
milk, to glaze
1 level tblsp sesame seeds, for topping

1. Beat together the pumpkin purée and margarine until soft.
2. Beat together the sugar, water and egg, sprinkle on the dried yeast and leave in a warm place for 10-15 minutes to become frothy.
3. Sift the flour, salt and spices, make a well in the centre and pour in the pumpkin purée and yeast liquid. Stir in the sultanas. Stir well and knead for 5 minutes, until the dough is smooth and leaves the sides of the bowl.
4. Wrap the dough loosely in greased polythene and leave in a warm place for about 1 hour, until it has doubled in size.
5. Turn out the dough and knead lightly to release air bubbles. Shape into a 9 inch (23 cm) round and place on a greased and warmed baking sheet. Cover loosely with greased polythene and leave in a warm place for about 45 minutes, to double in size again.
6. Bake in the oven at 400°F (200°C), Gas 6 for 30 minutes. Brush the top with milk and sprinkle with the sesame seeds. Return to the oven for 10 minutes, or until the loaf is firm and the top crusty.

FRUIT SALADS

A medley of two or more fruits, refreshingly chilled and attractively presented, can be the perfect way to enjoy both our own home produce and the dazzling array of imports from around the world.

Making a salad of fruits gives you the chance to choose types which contrast well with each other in terms of texture — crisp, sharp apples with soft, juicy peaches and nectarines; shape — sliced pears with cubes of watermelon, and fat, round black cherries; and colour. A salad of apples, green (or 'white') grapes, oranges and blackberries ranges from almost white to shiny black. Or it can be effective and fun to serve salads in a single colour theme — pale greens, a range of the red soft fruits, or the sunshine shades of mangoes, paw paw (or papaya), oranges or apricots.

Always remember to toss apples, pears, peaches and quinces in lemon juice or water acidulated with the juice as soon as you slice them; bananas too, but these are best added at the last minute. All these fruits quickly discolour on exposure to air.

Almost every fruit salad needs a 'syrup', the equivalent to the dressing in savoury salads, to mellow and link the flavours and provide a moist sauce. The strong movement away from additional sweetness, and particularly refined sugars, could herald the demise of the conventional caster sugar and water syrup. Tasty alternatives are unsweetened pineapple, orange or apple juice — I specially like the cloudy kind — flavoured perhaps with a sprig of rosemary or a couple of bay leaves. You can add or substitute cider, fortified and table wines, a spoonful of spirit or liqueur, or go the whole hog and serve strawberries and peaches floating in bubbly champagne.

Floating? Apples, pears, peaches, strawberries and bananas float. Grapes, oranges and canned fruits steeped in syrup are the salad sinkers.

Pineapple Romanoff
Serves 6

1 medium pineapple
8 oz (225 g) strawberries, hulled
4 oz (100 g) black grapes, seeded
juice of 1 lemon
grated rind and juice of 1 orange
¼ pt (150 ml) sweet white wine
1 oz (25 g) caster sugar, if needed

1. Cut the pineapple in half through the centre of the leaves and fruit. Cut away the flesh, taking care not to pierce the skin. Put the shells in the refrigerator to chill. Discard the hard core of the pineapple and cut the flesh into cubes.

2. Stir the pineapple, strawberries and grapes together. Mix the lemon juice, orange rind and juice, wine and sugar if needed and pour over the fruit. Stir, cover and chill.

3. To serve, pile the fruit into the pineapple shells, making sure to show off some of the best strawberries and some grapes on the top.

All-year-round Salad
Serves 6

2 dessert apples, peeled, cored and thinly sliced
2 dessert pears, peeled, cored and thinly sliced
2 level tblsp lemon juice
2 oranges, segmented
4 oz (100 g) black grapes, seeded
4 oz (100 g) white grapes, seeded
2 bananas

Syrup
3 oz (75 g) sugar
½ pt pt (275 ml) water
1 level tblsp lemon juice
1 level tblsp sweet sherry
1 bay leaf

1. Bring the syrup ingredients slowly to the boil, stirring to dissolve the sugar. Simmer for 3-4 minutes then cool. Discard the bay leaf.
2. As you slice the apples and pears, drop them into a small bowl of water acidulated with the lemon juice. This will prevent them from discolouring.
3. Drain the apples and pears and toss them with the oranges and grapes. Pour on the cooled syrup and toss carefully to avoid breaking the fruit. Cover and chill.
4. Just before serving, stir in the banana.

*When black or red cherries are available, they can colourfully replace the green grapes. Always stone them first — a small hand tool, a special cherry stoner, is the least messy way to do it, and leaves the fruit intact.

*If you wish to avoid added sugar, bring ½ pt (275 ml) cloudy unsweetened apple juice to the boil with a bay leaf and 1 level tablespoon lemon juice. Cool and discard the herb.

Fresh Date Spokewheel

Serves 4

8 oz (225 g) dried apricots, soaked and drained
¼ pt (150 ml) unsweetened orange juice
1 small sprig rosemary
3 oranges, segmented
12 fresh dates, stoned

1. Poach the apricots in the orange juice over low heat with the rosemary for 15 minutes. Cool, then discard the herb. Lift out the apricots with a draining spoon, reserving the juice.
2. Peel and segment the oranges. Add any escaping juice to the apricot liquid.
3. To arrange the salad, make a wheel pattern of the orange segments on a serving plate with the apricots around the outside. Pour over the fruit juice. Arrange the dates in the centre. Cover and leave for at least 30 minutes.

Dried Fruits in Cider

Serves 4

½ pt (275 ml) dry cider
1 level tblsp lemon juice
2 inch (5 cm) piece cinnamon
12 oz (350 g) mixed dried fruits — apple rings, apricots, peaches, pears, prunes
¼ pt (150 ml) plain low-fat yoghurt
2-3 drops cinnamon essence
2 tblsp blanched almonds, toasted

1. Bring the cider, lemon juice and cinnamon to the boil and simmer for 5 minutes.
2. Pour the hot cider over the fruit, cover and leave to macerate for at least 4 hours. Discard the cinnamon stick.
3. Beat the yoghurt and cinnamon essence and swirl over the fruit to serve. Scatter with the almonds. Serve at room temperature — not chilled.

Red Fruit Salad

Serves 6

2 large peaches, skinned, stoned and sliced
4 oz (100 g) raspberries, hulled
4 oz (100 g) loganberries, hulled
4 oz (100 g) strawberries, hulled
4 oz (100 g) redcurrants
4 oz (100 g) red cherries, stoned

Syrup
½ pt (275 ml) unsweetened orange juice
3 level tblsp clear honey
1 vanilla pod

1. Bring the orange juice, honey and vanilla pod slowly to the boil. Cool, then remove the vanilla pod. (Wash and dry it, and store for future use.)
2. Toss all the fruits together, pour on the syrup, cover and chill. Sprays of scented geranium leaves, or better still a couple of red nasturtium or gladioli flowers, finish off the dish well.

Burgundy Bananas

Serves 4

7 fl oz (200 ml) red wine
1 oz (25 g) Demerara sugar
1 inch (2.5 cm) piece cinnamon
a pinch of ground ginger
8 oz (225 g) black grapes, seeded and peeled
5 large bananas, cut slantwise into 2 inch (5 cm) pieces

1. Bring the wine, sugar, cinnamon and ginger slowly to the boil, stirring to dissolve the sugar.
2. Add the grapes and simmer for 3 minutes.
3. Pour the hot wine and grapes over the bananas and leave to cool. Discard the cinnamon. Serve cool but not chilled.

*This is a 'same-day' recipe — the bananas soften and start fraying at the edges if they are prepared more than an hour or so ahead.

Oranges in Yoghurt

Serves 4

6 oranges
2 oz (50 g) seedless raisins
2 level tblsp slivered almonds

Dressing
½ pt (275 ml) plain low-fat yoghurt
2 level tblsp clear honey
1 level tsp grated orange rind
1 level tblsp orange liqueur

1. Peel the oranges, taking care to remove every trace of the white pith. Very thinly slice them — an electric carving knife makes a superb job of it — and discard any seeds.

2. Scatter the raisins over the orange slices and any juice.
3. Mix all the dressing ingredients.
4. Pour the dressing over the oranges and very carefully toss them, without breaking.
5. Cover and chill for at least 30 minutes. Scatter with the almonds to decorate.

Hot Summer Salad

Serves 4

6 level tblsp unsweetened orange juice
3 level tblsp water
3 scented geranium leaves
1 level tblsp redcurrant jelly
1 lb (450 g) dessert gooseberries, topped and tailed
4 oz (100 g) redcurrants
8 oz (225 g) raspberries, hulled

1. Bring the orange juice, water, geranium leaves and jelly slowly to the boil in a wide pan.
2. Add the prepared fruit, shake the pan well and bring very slowly to the boil. Take care not to let the fruit collapse.
3. Discard the geranium leaves and serve hot. Though of course it's equally delicious cold.

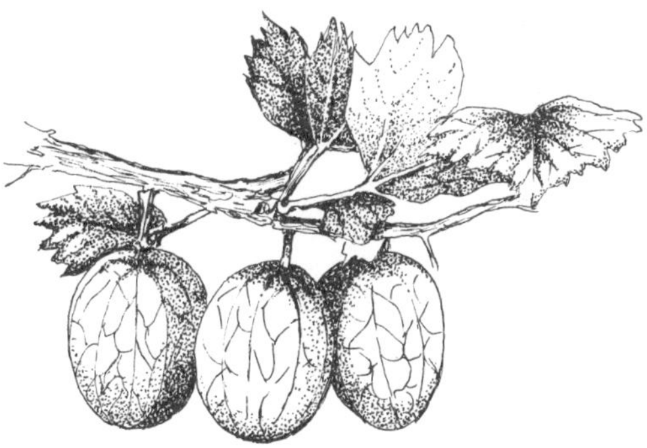

Green Fruit Salad

Serves 6

4 kiwi fruit
1 ogen melon
4 large, ripe greengages, stoned and sliced
4 oz (100 g) seedless green grapes, or white grapes, seeded and peeled
2 green dessert apples, cored and thinly sliced

Syrup
3 oz (75 g) sugar
½ pt (275 ml) water
2 level tblsp lemon juice
2 bay leaves

1. To make the syrup, stir the ingredients over low heat to dissolve the sugar, then bring to the boil and boil for 5 minutes. Leave to cool, then discard the bay leaves.
2. Cut the ends from the kiwi fruit. Using a very sharp potato peeler or small knife, peel away the brown skin. (With very ripe fruit or a medium-sharp tool, the skin may drag.)
3. Halve the melon and scoop out the seeds. Using a small vegetable baller, scoop out the spheres of the flesh as close together as possible. Save the juice to add to the syrup.
4. Mix all the fruits together and pour on the syrup. Cover and chill for at least 30 minutes.

*If you prefer a low-sugar 'syrup' simply macerate the fruits in clear or cloudy unsweetened apple juice sharpened with a little lemon or lime juice.

West Indian Fruit Bowl

Serves 6

1 mango, peeled, stoned and thinly sliced
1 paw paw, peeled, seeded and thinly sliced
1 small pineapple, skinned, cored and diced
2 oranges, segmented
1 level tblsp lemon juice
¼ pt (150 ml) water
2 level tblsp crème de menthe
1 banana, sliced
1 lime or lemon, thinly sliced, to decorate

1. Mix together all the fruit except the banana.
2. Mix the lemon juice, water and crème de menthe, pour over the fruit and stir.
3. Cover and chill for at least 1 hour.
4. Stir in the banana just before serving. Garnish with twists of lime or lemon.

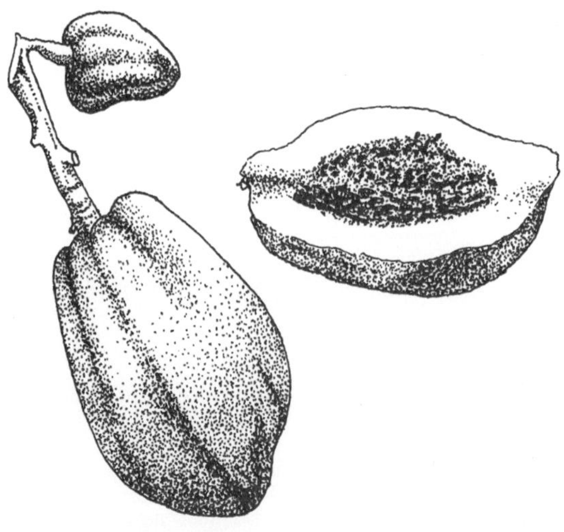

Oriental Orange Cocktail

Serves 6

3 oranges, sliced
12 fresh lychees
2 kiwi fruit, peeled and thinly sliced
2 bananas, sliced

Syrup
½ pt (275 ml) fresh orange juice
1 level tsp lemon juice
a strip of thinly pared orange rind
2 level tblsp orange liqueur, or orange wine

1. Thinly pare the rind of 1 orange and reserve. Peel the oranges, removing every trace of white pith. Thinly slice the oranges, using an electric carving knife if you have one.
2. Peel the lychees and kiwi fruit, using a very sharp knife or a rotating potato peeler. Slice the fruits.
3. To make the syrup, bring the orange juice and lemon juice to the boil with the orange rind, then leave to cool. Discard the orange rind and stir in the liqueur or wine.
4. Toss together the sliced oranges, lychees, kiwi fruit and bananas and pour over the syrup.

PUDDINGS

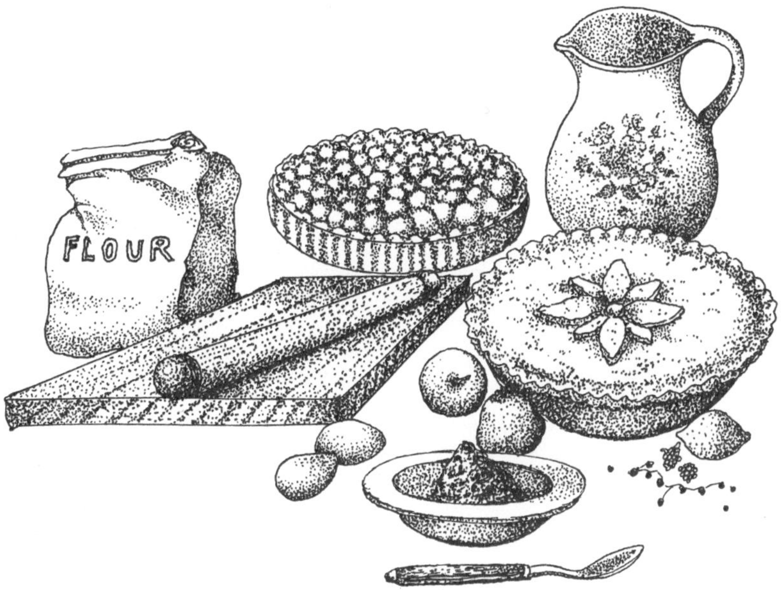

Ice-box cold or piping hot, the pudding course can present fruits summer-cool and at their most refreshing, or winter-cosy and at their most satisfying.

Fresh fruits that have a short season or may be picked on a day's countryside excursion — bilberries, mulberries, Cape gooseberries — are best served simply.

There is no doubt that dairy dishes of all kinds complement them deliciously. There is yoghurt, of course, and health-food enthusiasts will be deeply into making their own. Two French specialities are *crème fraîche,* double cream 'set' with cultured buttermilk and *cremets* in which the cream is lightened with beaten egg whites. Lower in calories, there's a recipe for a version of *coeur à la crème* made with cottage cheese. Mix and match these delicacies with the seasonal fruits as they appear.

Old favourites die hard; by substituting yoghurt for some or all of the cream in ice creams, using — less — Muscovado sugar in place of refined products and sweetening fancy fresh fruit with the natural sugars in dried fruits you can serve these desserts at least on highdays and holidays without too many pangs of conscience.

Chestnut Ice Cream
Serves 6

2 oz (50 g) seedless raisins
2 oz (50 g) sultanas
1 oz (25 g) chopped candied orange peel
1 oz (25 g) chopped candied citron peel
¼ pt (150 ml) Marsala, or sweet sherry
grated rind and juice of 1 orange
4 level tblsp water
2 oz (50 g) caster sugar
6 oz (150 g) unsweetened chestnut purée
½ pt (275 ml) plain low-fat yoghurt

1. Soak the raisins, sultanas and peel in the wine for 1 hour.
2. Bring the orange rind and juice, water and sugar slowly to the boil, stirring over low heat to dissolve the sugar. Simmer for 2 minutes.
3. Beat in the chestnut purée and leave to cool.
4. Beat in the yoghurt and stir in the fruit and wine.
5. Cover and freeze for 1 hour. Turn into a chilled bowl, beat thoroughly to break down the ice crystals, cover and freeze for a further 2 hours.
6. Allow the ice cream to rest in the refrigerator for 30-45 minutes before serving.

Cranberry and Cottage Cheese Ice Cream
Serves 6–8

6 oz (150 g) fresh or frozen cranberries, thawed
3 oz (75 g) caster sugar

2 level tblsp redcurrant jelly
1 lb (450 g) cottage cheese, sieved
¼ pt (150 ml) soured cream
¼ pt (150 ml) plain low-fat yoghurt
1 level tblsp lemon juice

1. Shake the cranberries in a pan over very low heat until they are soft. Stir in the sugar and jelly to dissolve. Cool.
2. Beat together the cottage cheese, soured cream, yoghurt and lemon juice and beat in the cranberries.
3. Turn the mixture into a chilled container such as an ice cube tray, cover and freeze for 3 hours. There is no need to beat it, as usual, at the half-frozen stage.
4. Soften the ice cream in the refrigerator for 45 minutes before serving. You can serve a purée of cranberries or melted redcurrant jelly as a sauce.

Frozen Passion Fruit 'Cream'

Serves 4

The dark orangey-green fruits you can buy in specialty greengrocers come from *Passiflora edulis,* a plant native to South America and recognized by their crinkly skins. They are much larger and sweeter than the garden variety, *P. coerulea,* which can be grown in Northern Europe. The imported fruit is always expensive in Britain. The flavour of passion fruits is so distinctive they are best served simply, and alone.

4 large passion fruits
3 oz (75 g) sugar
1 level tsp lemon juice
3½ fl oz (100 ml) water
¼ pt (150 ml) plain low-fat yoghurt

1. Cut off the tops of the passion fruit and scoop out the flesh and seeds.
2. Heat the sugar, lemon juice and water over low heat, stirring once or twice, until the sugar dissolves. Bring to the boil, simmer for 5 minutes then add the fruit and seeds. Simmer for no more than 2 minutes.
3. Sieve the fruit and leave the purée to cool. You can use a few of the seeds — which are chewy but edible — to decorate the dish.
4. Cover the cold purée and freeze for 1 hour. Beat it vigorously to break down the ice crystals, then beat in the yoghurt.
5. Cover and freeze again for 2 hours.
6. Leave to soften in the refrigerator for about 30 minutes before serving. Serve in ramekin dishes in small scoops made with a vegetable baller. Decorate with some washed and dried seeds. Langue au chat biscuits are a good accompaniment.

*You can of course use whipped double cream in place of the yoghurt for a richer dessert with a much 'fuller' flavour.

*Guava cream can be made in just the same way. Skin and simmer 3-4 guavas, depending on size, then sieve out the fat round seeds. Replace the lemon juice with the juice of 1 orange.

Iced Plum Soufflé

Serves 4

1 lb (450 g) plums or greengages
4 fl oz (125 ml) water
6 oz (150 g) sugar
3 large egg whites
½ pt (275 ml) double cream, whipped
3 level tblsp kirsch, or gin
a few fresh plums or greengages, to decorate

1. Simmer the plums in 2 level tablespoons of the water for 15 minutes, until they are tender. Sieve them to discard the stones and skins and cool the purée.
2. Dissolve the sugar in the remaining water over low heat, stirring frequently. Increase the heat and boil the syrup to a temperature of 248°F (120°C), the 'hard ball' stage. This means — a useful test if you haven't a sugar thermometer — that a small amount of the syrup dropped into water will quickly form a firm ball.
3. Whisk the egg whites until they are stiff.
4. Pour on the hot syrup and beat constantly.
5. Fold the whipped cream, liqueur and fruit purée into the meringue mixture.
6. Turn the dessert into a straight-sided soufflé dish, cover and freeze.
7. Transfer the dish to the refrigerator to soften for 30-45 minutes before serving.
8. For the decoration, halve, stone and then quarter the plums. Arrange them in a wheel pattern, cut sides up.

*You may prefer, for the sake of fat and cholesterol content, to substitute plain low-fat yoghurt for the cream.

*If you enjoy the melt-in-the-mouth frothiness of this dessert, make it with other fruit purées. It is specially good with dried apricot purée, apple lightly spiced with ginger, and rhubarb cooked with a cinnamon stick. The purée must not be too runny.

Watermelon Sorbet

Serves 6

There's nothing more refreshing than a slice of chilled watermelon, the bright sunset pink flesh outlined by the rim of dark green rind. Extend the season by turning some of the fruit into sorbet and, for the best of both worlds, serve a slice of fruit and a scoop of the perfectly complementary ice.

2 lb (900 g) watermelon
2 egg whites
a pinch of salt
a pinch of cream of tartar
2 level tblsp lemon juice
3 oz (75 g) caster sugar

1. Cut the watermelon from the rind. Discard the seeds, chop the flesh and liquidize it or press it through a sieve.
2. Cover and freeze for about 1 hour, until the pulp is mushy.
3. Whisk the egg whites, salt, cream of tartar, lemon juice and sugar over a pan of simmering water until it is stiff. Leave to cool.
4. Fold the meringue mixture into the partly frozen watermelon. Cover and freeze for 1 hour.
5. Turn the mixture into a chilled bowl, beat well to break down ice crystals, cover and freeze for a further 2 hours.
6. The meringue mixture holds air in the fruit, so there is no need to soften the sorbet in the refrigerator before serving. It's one iced dessert you *can* forget about till the last minute.

Bilberry Kissel with Junket
Serves 6

The slighty sharp flavour of these small bluish-black fruits puts them largely out of bounds if you are trying to cut sugar to a minimum. They grow abundantly in France, northern England and Scotland and have a variety of names: airelles, blaeberry, whortleberry and myrtle among them. They are perfectly partnered by creamy desserts of all kinds — *fromage blanc, crème fraîche, coeur à la crème* or, as here, plain everyday junket.

2lb (900 g) bilberries, stalks and leaves removed
2 oz (50 g) sugar
4 level tblsp clear honey
2 level tblsp orange juice
4 level tblsp water
a pinch of ground cinnamon
a pinch of grated nutmeg
3 level tblsp wholemeal flour

Junket
1 pt (575 ml) milk
2 level tsp caster sugar
2 level tblsp cooking brandy
1 level tsp liquid rennet

1. To make the junket, warm the milk to blood heat and add the sugar. Stir over low heat until it has dissolved. Stir in the brandy, remove from the heat and stir in the rennet.
2. Pour the junket into a serving bowl and leave it undisturbed at room temperature for 5-6 hours to set.
3. Put the bilberries, sugar, honey, orange juice, water and spices into a casserole, cover and cook gently over low heat for 15 minutes, stirring at first to dissolve the sugar.
4. Mix a little of the juice into the flour to make a paste. Pour into the fruit and bring slowly to the boil, stirring until the fruit thickens. Pour into a serving dish and leave to cool. Decorate both the junket and fruit kissel with herb leaves if possible. In the north of England mint is a traditional accompaniment to 'blaeberries'. I prefer scented geranium leaves.

*You can make kissel with a variety of other fruits; rhubarb, blackcurrants, raspberries and stoned and sieved plums.

Blackcurrant Tofu Whip

Serves 4

A 5 oz (125 g) packet of silken tofu is a compact way of taking natural high-quality vegetable protein and contains only about 65 calories. Made from soya beans, it is free of cholesterol and high in polyunsaturated fats. Tofu is however characteristically low on flavour and looks like a block of milky-white blancmange. Spark it up with the refreshing flavour of fresh or frozen soft fruits.

1 lb (450 g) fresh or frozen blackcurrants
3 level tblsp clear honey
3 level tblsp cassis sirop
5 oz (125 g) silken tofu

1. Reserve a few blackcurrants to decorate. Put the remainder in a pan with the honey and simmer over very low heat until the juice runs.

2. Liquidize in a blender with the sirop and tofu.

3. Pour into 4 individual serving glasses and chill. Decorate with the reserved currants.

Blueberry Cheesecake

Serves 6-8

Blueberries grow wild in both Europe and North America, where they are larger and sweeter. The fruits are like enlarged blackcurrents, dark bluish black and with a hazy 'bloom'. You can buy them frozen, canned and as a sweetened purée for a pie or pancake filling. They are a perfect colour and flavour contrast to the creamy cheesecake layer.

2 oz (50 g) margarine, melted
4 oz (100 g) digestive biscuits, crushed
12 oz (350 g) low-fat curd cheese
¼ pt (150 ml) plain low-fat yoghurt
2 eggs, separated
3 oz (75 g) sugar
1 level tsp vanilla essence
grated rind and juice of ½ lemon

Topping
1 lb (450 g) blueberries
3 level tblsp water
3 level tblsp clear honey
2 level tsp arrowroot

1. Mix the margarine and biscuits and press the mixture into the base of a greased 8 inch (20 cm) flan ring on a baking sheet.

2. Beat together the cheese, yoghurt, egg yolks, sugar, vanilla essence, lemon rind and juice.

3. Whisk the egg whites until they are stiff and fold into the mixture.

4. Pour into the flan ring and smooth the top. Make a ridge about ¼ inch (6 mm) wide and ½ inch (12 mm) deep all around, to leave a hollow for the fruit.

5. Bake in the oven at 375°F (190°C), Gas 5 for 35 minutes, when the top should be golden brown. Leave to cool.

6. Simmer the blueberries, water and honey over low heat for about 5 minutes until they soften — do not allow them to collapse.
7. Lift out the fruit with a draining spoon. Mix the arrowroot to a paste with a little of the juice, add to the remaining juice and bring to the boil, stirring. Boil until the juice thickens and becomes translucent. Cool slightly.
8. Spread the fruit over the cheesecake and pour on the glaze. Cool then chill the cheesecake.

*Blackcurrants and blackberries are good alternatives when blueberries are not available.

Mulberry Compote with Coeur à la Crème

Serves 4-6

2 lb (900 g) mulberries
about 2 oz (50 g) icing sugar

Coeur à la Crème
2 level tsp powdered gelatine
2 level tblsp hot water
12 oz (350 g) cottage cheese, sieved
5 oz (125 g) plain low-fat yoghurt

1. Begin the day before by making the slimmers' version of cream curds. Dissolve the gelatine in the hot water. Beat the cottage cheese and yoghurt together and beat in the gelatine mixture.
2. Turn the mixture into four 4 oz (100 g) cheese moulds, cover and leave in a dish in the refrigerator to drain overnight. No moulds? Use plastic yoghurt pots — they must not be narrower at the necks than the base, or the 'cheese' won't turn out. Tie muslin over the tops and invert them.
3. Select half of the mulberries, choosing the best specimens. Put the remainder in a pan over low heat until the juice runs. Liquidize in a blender, sieve, stir in the sugar and pour the juice over the whole fruit. Leave to cool, then chill.
4. Turn out the cheese moulds and serve with the mulberries.

Pears in Apricot Sauce

Serves 4

8 oz (225 g) dried apricots, soaked
2 inch (5 cm) piece cinnamon
thinly pared rind and juice of 1 orange
8 oz (225 g) dried pears, soaked and drained
2 oz (50 g) dried mulberries
4 level tblsp blanched almonds, toasted

1. Cook the apricots in the soaking water with the cinnamon, orange rind and juice for 20 minutes.
2. Discard the cinnamon and orange rind. Liquidize the apricots with ¼ pt (150 ml) of the liquid to make a smooth purée.
3. Cook the pears in the remaining liquid for 25 minutes, or until they are tender.
4. Drain the pears and stir them into the apricot sauce. Cool then chill.
5. To serve, scatter the dish with the mulberries and almonds. Plain yoghurt is a good accompaniment.

*Apricot sauce is marvellously versatile. Serve it, too, with poached fresh pears, dried apple rings or lightly stewed apples garnished with dates.

Quince and Apple Suedoise
Serves 6-8

Use only very ripe quinces, when the skins are bright yellow and the fruits scent the room. Even then they can be tough; you need a very sharp knife and peeler — and more time than it takes to prepare apples. Drop the fruit into water acidulated with extra lemon juice as you work.

3 oz (75 g) light Muscovado sugar
½ pt (275 ml) water
1 lemon, thinly pared
1 lb (450 g) quinces, peeled, cored and thinly sliced
1½ lb (725 g) cooking apples, peeled, cored and chopped
6 dried apricots, soaked and drained
¾ oz (20 g) powdered gelatine

1. Bring the sugar and water slowly to the boil, stirring over low heat. Add half the lemon rind and fast-boil for 3 minutes.

2. Add the quince slices and poach over low heat for 20-25 minutes, or until they are tender. Lift out the fruit with a draining spoon and fast-boil the syrup for 5 minutes.

3. Add the remaining lemon rind, the juice of the lemon, chopped apples and apricots to the syrup. Simmer uncovered, stirring often, until the apples collapse. Discard the lemon rind and sieve or liquidize the fruit in a blender.

4. Dissolve the gelatine in a little hot water and stir into the apple purée. Beat well. Set aside to cool.

5. Rinse out a 2 pt (1 litre) ring mould with cold water. Arrange the quince slices in a pattern.

6. Spoon in cold apple purée, taking care not to jumble the quince slices. Leave in the refrigerator for about 3 hours to set.

7. Unmould and serve in slices with *fromage blanc* or *crème fraîche* (below).

* Instead of quinces to decorate the mould and flavour the syrup you can use nectarines. Quarter 3 large ones, simmer them and then skin them — the skins will tint the syrup pink.

Cape Gooseberries with Crème Fraîche

Imported Cape gooseberries (also known as goldenberries) are available — at a price! — in winter. They are an edible variety, *Physalis peruviana,* of the familiar garden plant known as Chinese lanterns. The small, round yellowish green fruits, too, are encased in web-like calyces. As they are so spectacular they are best enjoyed in this form. Cut the calyces open like petals of a flower. Guests can twist out the fruit.

16-20 Cape gooseberries

Crème Fraîche
½ pt (275 ml) double cream
1 level tblsp cultured buttermilk

1. Make the *crème fraîche* the day before. It will keep, covered, in the refrigerator for up to 2 weeks. Have both ingredients at warm room temperature. Stir the buttermilk into the cream, cover and leave in a warm room overnight, then chill.

2. To prepare the Cape gooseberries slit the calyces from the tip almost to the base in 4 places, using small, sharp scissors. Open out the sections, like flower petals, to reveal the fruit. Arrange them on a plate.

3. Serve the *crème fraîche* in bowls, with the goldenberries as a sweetmeat, on side plates.

Dried Fruit Fool with Cremets

Serves 6

8 oz (225 g) prunes, soaked and drained
¼ pt (150 ml) red wine
2 inch (5 cm) piece cinnamon
6 oz (150 g) seedless raisins
½ pt (275 ml) strained tea
1 level tblsp lemon juice
12 walnut halves

Cremets
½ pt (275 ml) double cream
3 large egg whites

1. Begin the day before, by making the *cremets.* Whip the cream until it is very stiff. Whisk the egg whites and fold them in. Turn the mixture into 6 draining moulds or improvise with wide-necked yoghurt pots. Tie muslin over the necks, invert on a dish and leave to drain overnight. Turn out on to a dish to serve.
2. Put the prunes, wine and cinnamon in a covered casserole and cook in the oven at 325°F (170°C), Gas 3 for 1½ hours.
3. Put the raisins in another covered dish with the tea and cook in the oven at 325°F (170°C), Gas 3 for 1 hour.
4. Discard the cinnamon and liquidize the prunes and wine.
5. Pour off the tea and liquidize the raisins with the lemon juice.
6. Mix together the two purées. Pour into a serving dish and chill. Decorate the top with walnut halves and serve with a portion of *cremets.*

* You can make an up-dated and down-caloried *cremets* with plain low-fat yoghurt. Whip the yoghurt, fold in the whisked egg whites and drain. The result will inevitably be much 'thinner'. But then so will you!

Figgy Pudding

Serves 6

4 oz (100 g) wholewheat self-raising flour
1 level tsp baking powder
1 level tsp ground ginger
4 oz (100 g) light Muscovado sugar
4 oz (100 g) soft margarine
2 large eggs, lightly beaten
5 oz (125 g) dried figs, chopped
2 level tblsp clear honey

Sauce
3 level tblsp clear honey
1 level tblsp lemon juice
3 level tblsp water
1 level tblsp dark rum (optional)
4 oz (100 g) dried figs, chopped

1. This is a quick-mix pudding. Beat together the flour, baking powder, ginger, sugar, margarine and eggs until the mixture is smooth. Stir in the figs.
2. Pour the honey into the base of a greased 1½ pt (1 litre) pudding basin. Pour in the mixture, cover with foil and a cloth and tie.
3. Steam the pudding on a trivet over boiling water for 1¾ hours, topping up with more water as necessary.
4. Heat all the sauce ingredients over low heat, stirring to dissolve the honey. Simmer gently for 5 minutes.
5. Turn out the pudding and serve the sauce separately.

Nectarine and Apricot Pancakes

Makes 8 pancakes

I created this recipe for the launch of a new range of non-stick frying-pans, to show that — in a high-quality product — even pancakes can be cooked without any oil or fat.

4 oz (100 g) wholewheat flour
1 level tblsp caster sugar
1 egg, beaten
¼ pt (150 ml) orange juice
¼ pt (150 ml) soda water
icing sugar, to dust
½ pt (275 ml) plain low-fat yoghurt
2 level tblsp apricot liqueur

Filling
4 nectarines, skinned, stoned and thinly sliced
1 level tblsp lemon juice
2 level tblsp apricot liqueur
½ pt (275 ml) dried apricot purée

1. Make a batter with the flour, sugar, egg, orange juice and soda water.
2. Heat a good-quality non-stick frying-pan over moderate heat. If necessary, smear the base with oil. Pour in enough batter to cover the base with a thin film. Cook the pancake on one side, flip or toss and cook the other side. Keep the pancakes warm while you cook the remainder.
3. Toss the nectarine slices in lemon juice. Stir the apricot liqueur into the purée and spread the mixture over the pancakes.
4. Reserve 8 nectarine slices to decorate and fill the pancakes with the remainder. Fold each pancake in half and then in half again, envelope style.
5. Arrange the pancakes in a flameproof dish, dust with icing sugar and flash under a hot grill. Decorate with the reserved nectarine slices. Serve with the yoghurt flavoured with the liqueur.

Baked Pears

Serves 6

6 large, ripe dessert pears
3 oz (75 g) seedless raisins
3 oz (75 g) chopped, mixed nuts
2 pieces preserved ginger, finely chopped
4 level tblsp clear honey
¼ pt (150 ml) dry white wine
1 level tblsp ginger syrup

1. Cut a slice from the top of each pear. Using an apple corer, cut out a channel larger than the core itself.
2. Mix together the raisins, nuts, chopped ginger and half the honey and pack into the pear cavities. Place the pears upright in a baking dish which just fits them.
3. Bring the remaining honey, the wine and ginger syrup to the boil. Pour over the pears and cover with foil.
4. Bake in the oven at 375°F (190°C), Gas 5 for 25 minutes, basting occasionally with the syrup. If you prefer a thicker sauce, pour off the liquid and fast-boil it to a syrupy consistency. Serve hot. Chilled yoghurt makes a good accompaniment.

Apple Pie with Bramble Sauce

Serves 6

8 oz (225 g) wholewheat flour
salt
½ level tsp ground cinnamon
4 oz (100 g) margarine
2 level tblsp cold water
1½ lb (700 g) cooking apples, peeled, cored and thinly sliced
grated rind and juice of 1 orange
3 oz (75 g) macadamia nuts, roughly chopped
1 egg white, lightly beaten

Sauce
8 oz (225 g) cooking apples, peeled, cored and roughly chopped
2 level tblsp water
½ oz (15 g) margarine
1 oz (25 g) light Muscovado sugar
8 oz (225 g) blackberries

1. Sift the flour, salt and cinnamon and tip in the bran from the sieve. Rub in the margarine until the mixture is like crumbs. Mix to a dough with the water. Cover and chill for 30 minutes.
2. Roll out on a lightly floured board and use two-thirds of the pastry to line a greased 8 inch (20 cm) pie case.
3. Toss the apple slices in the orange rind and juice and arrange them in the pie case. Sprinkle with the nuts.
4. Dampen the edges and cover with the remaining pastry. Trim and decorate the edges. Brush the top with the egg white. Cut decorative shapes with the trimmings, arrange them on the pie and brush with egg white. Make a small hole in the top to allow steam to escape.
5. Bake in the oven at 425°F (220°C), Gas 7 for 30 minutes, until the pastry is crisp and deep, golden brown. Serve warm, with the sauce.
6. To make the sauce, simmer the apples with the water until they are soft. Beat in the margarine and sugar and stir in the blackberries. Simmer very gently for 3-4 minutes. Serve warm.

Steamed Carrot Pudding

Serves 4

The carrots and dried fruits provide so much sweetness that there's no need for extra sugar. This is an interesting alternative to Christmas pudding.

2 oz (50 g) wholewheat flour
2 oz (50 g) wholewheat breadcrumbs
3 oz (75 g) grated carrot
1 oz (25 g) ground almonds
1 level tsp ground cinnamon
grated rind and juice of 1 orange
2 eggs, separated
2 oz (50 g) sultanas
2 oz (50 g) dried mulberries
2 oz (50 g) hazelnuts, roughly chopped

1. Mix together the flour, crumbs, carrot, ground almonds, cinnamon and orange rind. Stir in the orange juice, egg yolks, dried fruit and nuts and beat well. Whisk the egg whites until stiff and fold them in.
2. Turn the mixture into a greased 1½ pt (900 ml) basin, cover with foil or a cloth and tie.
3. Steam the pudding on a trivet over boiling water for 2 hours, topping up with more water as needed.
4. Turn out the pudding and serve it hot. Soured cream is specially good with it, though yoghurt is better for the conscience.

Coconut Apples with Yoghurt Custard

Serves 4

4 large cooking apples, peeled and cored
8 dried apricots, chopped, soaked and drained
2 level tblsp macadamia nuts, or hazelnuts, roughly chopped
1 egg white, beaten
3 level tblsp desiccated coconut

Custard
½ pt (275 ml) plain low-fat yoghurt
2 eggs, beaten
1 level tblsp light Muscovado sugar
1 vanilla pod

1. Fill the apple cavities with the apricots and nuts. Roll the apples in first the egg white and then the coconut.
2. Stand the apples in a greased baking dish and cook in the oven at 325°F (170°C), Gas 3 for 1 hour, or until they are tender.
3. To make the custard, beat the yoghurt with the eggs and sugar. Pour into a baking dish and add the vanilla pod.
4. Stand the dish in a larger one with water to come half-way up the sides and cook in the oven with the apples.

Cherry Clafouti

Serves 4

1½ oz (40 g) wholewheat flour
salt
1½ oz (40 g) light Muscovado sugar
a large pinch of ground cinnamon
2 eggs, separated
1 extra egg yolk
1 level tblsp vegetable oil
½ pt (275 ml) milk
1½ lb (700 g) fresh cherries, stoned
caster sugar, to dust (optional)

1. Mix the flour, salt, sugar and cinnamon. Beat in the egg yolks and oil and gradually beat in the milk. Stiffly whisk the egg whites and fold them into the batter.
2. Arrange the cherries in a greased baking dish and pour on the batter.
3. Bake in the oven at 350°F (180°C), Gas 4 for 40-45 minutes, until the batter is firm and well risen. Serve hot.

*Reserve one or two bunches of fresh cherries to decorate the dish.

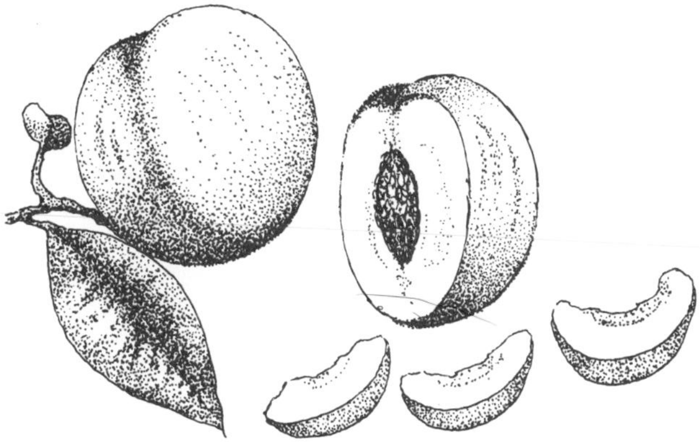

Peach Jelly with Ricotta Veil
Serves 6

2 lb (900 g) peaches
2 oz (50 g) caster sugar
½ pt (275 ml) water
½ pt (275 ml) dry sherry
1 level tblsp ginger syrup
1 level tblsp powdered gelatine

Topping
4 oz (100 g) ricotta cheese
¼ pt (150 ml) plain low-fat yoghurt
2 level tblsp icing sugar
2 level tblsp apricot liqueur
2 oz (50 g) toasted almonds

1. Put the sugar and the water in a frying pan and stir over low heat to dissolve, then add the sherry and ginger syrup. Bring to just below boiling point.

2. Add the peaches and simmer very gently for 2-3 minutes, rolling the fruit over in the syrup.

3. Leave the fruit in the syrup to cool. Skin, stone and slice the peaches and arrange them in a serving dish.

4. Dissolve the gelatine in a little hot water. Boil the syrup to reduce it by one-third. Pour the gelatine into the syrup and mix well.

5. Pour the gelatine mixture over the peaches, cool and chill.

6. Mix together the cheese, yoghurt, icing sugar and liqueur. Spread over the fruit, level the top and sprinkle with the nuts.

Coriander Plum Dowdy
Serves 4-6

6 thin slices day-old bread, cut from a large loaf
low-fat spread
8 oz (225 g) cooking apples, peeled, cored and sliced
1 lb (450 g) plums or greengages, stoned and halved
4 level tblsp light Muscovado sugar
1 level tsp coriander seeds
½ level tsp ground coriander

1. Cut the crusts from the bread and spread each slice on one side with the low-fat spread.

2. Line a greased 2 pt (1 litre) pie dish with the bread, spread side down. Cover with the apple and plums or greengages and sprinkle with the coriander seeds and half the sugar. Cover with the remaining bread, spread side up. Sprinkle with the remaining sugar mixed with the coriander.

3. Bake in the oven at 375F (190°C), Gas 5 for 1-1¼ hours, until the bread topping is crisp. Serve hot.

Snapdragons

Serves 6

Raisins in brandy are a traditional sweetmeat at Hallowe'en, when a game of 'chicken' was sometimes played. Guests were — ill advisedly — dared to snatch the raisins from the flames. Muscatels are the best raisins for this dish but they must be seeded, and that's a tedious job.

1 lb (450 g) seedless raisins
3½ fl oz (100 ml) orange juice
3½ fl oz (100 ml) cooking brandy
2 inch (5 cm) piece cinnamon
soured cream or vanilla ice cream, to serve

1. Soak the raisins in the orange juice for at least 1 hour.
2. Stir in the brandy and cinnamon and soak for a further 1 hour. Remove the cinnamon.
3. Set light to the raisins as you bring them to the table, a flicker of purplish blue flames. Serve very hot with chilled cream to contrast.

DRINKS

When it comes to drinks, fruit has something to offer us at all times of day, on all occasions and in all moods.

To start the day with a zing there are 'vitality' drinks, today's equivalent of milk shakes, of chilled yoghurt, buttermilk or skimmed milk whizzed up in a blender with soaked and drained dried fruits and any fresh fruit you care to mention. By adding wheatgerm, bran and nuts you can make the glass more health-giving still.

When it's time to celebrate there's a sparkling idea for strawberries bobbing in a bowl of wine you can choose other soft or sliced fruits too, of course — and when the north wind doth blow you can borrow a leaf from grandfather's book and serve fruit-flavoured mulled wine. We have some recipes for a heart-warming concoction based on blackcurrant purée and another for port and lemon mull which features baked lemon, an interesting way of intensifying the flavour.

Lemon Barley Water

Makes 1⅔ pints (1 litre)

A summer pick-you-up.

2 oz (50 g) pearl barley, washed and drained
1½ pt (850 ml) water
thinly pared rind and juice of 3 lemons
2 oz (50 g) freshly ground almonds
2 level tsp clear honey

1. Pour the barley, water, lemon rind, almonds and honey into a pan and bring slowly to the boil. Simmer until the mixture thickens.
2. Strain, pressing out all the liquid. Add the lemon juice and mix well.
3. Pour into sterilized bottles, cover and store in a cool place.
4. To serve, dilute with water and ice cubes and decorate with twists of lemon peel, thin slices of lemon or mint sprigs.

Peach Sunset

Serves 4

A 'vitality' drink to pep you up first thing in the morning, or throughout the day.

6 oz (150 g) dried peaches, soaked
½ pt (275 ml) plain low-fat yoghurt, chilled
1 can concentrated frozen orange juice, thawed
grated rind and juice of 1 orange
1 level tblsp wheatgerm
2 level tblsp blanched almonds, roughly chopped

1. Whizz in a blender the peaches, ¼ pt (150 ml) of the soaking water and other ingredients (except the almonds) to make a light, frothy foam.
2. Pour into chilled glasses or pottery beakers and top with the almonds.

Strawberry Shake

Serves 4

More refreshing than a cup of tea to drink on a hot day in the garden, or take in a flask for a picnic.

12 oz (350 g) strawberries, hulled
½ pt (275 ml) plain low-fat yoghurt, chilled
3 level tblsp clear honey
mint leaves or borage flowers, to decorate

1. Reserve 4 of the best strawberries to decorate. Chop one third of the fruit and set aside.
2. Whizz the remaining strawberries with the yoghurt and honey. Stir in the chopped fruit.
3. Serve in chilled glasses, decorate with the reserved fruit and the herbs.

Strawberry Sparkle
Makes 8-12 drinks

½ pt (275 ml) crushed ice
4 dashes Angostura bitters
1¼ pt (700 ml) bottle rosé vermouth, chilled
1 miniature bottle strawberry liqueur
rind of 1 orange
1¼ pt (700 ml) sparkling mineral water, chilled
8 oz (225 g) strawberries, sliced

1. In a chilled jug or serving bowl, pour the bitters, vermouth and liqueur over the ice. Add the orange rind, cover and leave for 1 hour.
2. Pour on the mineral water, stir well and discard the orange peel.
3. Float the strawberries on top and serve in chilled glasses.

Blackcurrant Punch
Makes about 4 pints (2.3 litres)

An unusual 'mull' to serve on a cold winter's night. It's a great party opener.

½ pt (275 ml) blackcurrant purée
thinly pared rind and juice of 2 lemons
1 bottle dry red wine
¼ pt (150 ml) sweet sherry
2 pt (1 litre) hot water
2 oz (50 g) caster sugar
1 orange stuck with 6 whole cloves
thin slices of orange, to serve

1. Heat all the ingredients slowly together, stirring over low heat to dissolve the purée and sugar. Bring to just below boiling point but do not allow to boil.
2. Serve in heated glasses decorated with a slice of orange.

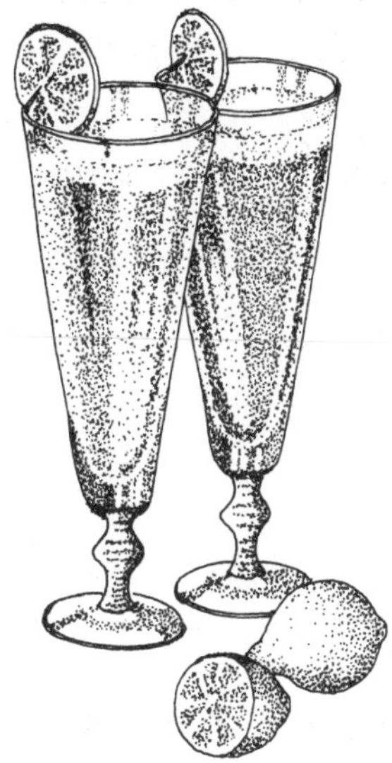

Caribbean Cup
Makes 4 glasses

The concept is exotic but the ingredients take account of the calorie content.

4 passion fruits
4 fl oz (125 ml) frozen concentrated orange juice, thawed
1 pt (575 ml) skimmed milk, chilled

1. Halve the passion fruits and scoop out the flesh and seeds. Pour on the orange juice and milk and stir well.
2. Sieve to remove the seeds.
3. Serve in chilled glasses. Tiny Japanese paper umbrellas make a pretty decoration for each glass.

Port and Lemon Mull

Makes 12 glasses

This is a 'roaring log fire on a windy night' drink, a perfect greeting at the start of a party.

8 cloves
2 lemons
1¼ pt (700 ml) port
1¼ pt (700 ml) water
1 stick cinnamon
a few blades of mace
12 lumps sugar

1. Stick the cloves into 1 of the lemons and heat in the oven at 350°F (180°C), Gas 4 for 15 minutes. This intensifies the flavours.
2. Heat the port to just below boiling point — do not let it boil.
3. Boil the water with the cinnamon and mace and simmer for 5 minutes.
4. Add the water and baked lemon to the port.
5. Rub the sugar lumps over the rim of the second lemon to extract the juices in the skin.
6. Put the sugar in a heatproof bowl and pour on the heated wine mixture and the juice of the lemon and stir well. Serve hot in heated or heatproof glasses.

Banana Flip

Serves 4

4 ripe bananas
1 pt (575 ml) unsweetened pineapple juice, chilled
4 eggs
4 level tblsp sweet sherry
4 level tblsp single cream
lemon slices, to serve

1. Whizz all the ingredients (except the lemon slices) to make a smooth foam. Serve well chilled, with lemon slices to decorate.

Blackcurrant Yoghurt

Makes about 1 pint (575 ml).

4 oz (100 g) blackcurrants
2 level tblsp sugar
½ pt (275 ml) plain low-fat yoghurt
¼ pt (150 ml) skimmed milk

1. Put the blackcurrants and sugar into a blender, add a little of the yoghurt and blend until smooth. Add the remaining yoghurt and the milk and blend thoroughly. Serve chilled.

PRESERVES

Preserving fruit is one of the most satisfying and homely of pastimes, directly descended from the early homesteaders who had to make the fruits of one harvest keep in perfect condition the year around.

With modern methods of storage and access to fruits from all over the world we no longer have this need. It is a great compliment to earlier generations of cooks, therefore, that preserving has survived at all.

These recipes are only a taste of the endless possibilities. Dried apple rings really for old times' sake; but it's a practical and economic way to treat a glut of fruit in the garden or take advantage of low prices in the shops. And, a great advantage, it's one way of preserving fruit without adding sugar.

Kumquats in Brandy

Fills two 1 lb (450 g) jars

These small, round members of the orange family make fabulous preserves to give as a special present or serve, sparingly, with cold meat, game or poultry.

1 lb (450 g) kumquats, washed and dried
4 level tblsp sugar
2 inch (5 cm) piece of cinnamon
about ½ pt (275 ml) cooking brandy

1. Prick the kumquats all over with a darning needle.
2. Pack them into dry, sterilized jars, sprinkling sugar between each layer. Split the cinnamon stick lengthways and push a piece into each jar.
3. Fill the jars with the brandy so that the top of the fruit is covered.
4. Cover with non-corrosive lids such as plastic-lined screw-on caps. Shake the jars to dissolve the sugar. Label and store in a cool, dry place for 6 months.

Dried Apple Rings

This is the way to dry and store your own apple harvest. Bramleys are particularly good.

1. Peel and core the apples and cut away any blemishes — the slightest speck or bruise will be damaging.
2. Cut into ¼ inch (6 mm) thick rings and drop them at once into salted water. Use 1 oz (25 g) salt to 4 pt (2.3 litres) water.
3. Drain the apples and thread them on (ideally) new bamboo garden canes over a deep baking tin.
4. Dry the fruit in the warming drawer, or in the oven at the lowest temperature — it must not exceed 140°F (66°C). If necessary leave the oven door slightly ajar. Turn the apples occasionally until they are as dry as chamois leather. Depending on the juiciness of the fruit, this will take 4-6 hours. Test by pressing with a fingernail. The rings should resist pressure and no juice should ooze out.
5. Remove the fruit from the oven and leave for 12 hours in a dry, warm place.
6. To store, pack in airtight jars or tins.
7. To use the rings, soak them for at least 12 hours — longer than is needed for commercially prepared ones.

Pickled Limes

Fills two 1 lb (450 g) jars

Here's a way to capture this elusive fruit when the price in the shops comes down. Serve with fish or grilled meat.

6 limes, thinly sliced
4 level tblsp block salt
½ level tsp paprika
about ½ pt (275 ml) vegetable oil such as sunflower or peanut oil

1. Spread the limes on a wire cooling rack standing on a tray. Sprinkle them with salt and leave for 24 hours.
2. Wash and drain the fruit and pack into sterilized jars, sprinkling paprika between each layer.
3. Pour on the oil to cover the fruit. Cover with non-corrosive screw or clip-on lids and leave for 4 weeks before using.
4. Take out the slices you need with a draining spoon. The oil that is left can be used to make salad dressings and for cooking.

Pear and Ginger Chutney

Makes 5-6 lb (2.3-2.8 kg)

3 cloves garlic, crushed
salt (about 1 level tblsp)
grated rind and juice of 1 lemon
10 oz (300 g) molasses sugar
2 pt (1.1 litres) cider vinegar
3½ lb (1.7 kg) cooking pears, peeled, cored and chopped
1 lb (450 g) onions, chopped
12 oz (350 g) seedless raisins
8 oz (225 g) cooking apples, peeled, cored and chopped
4 oz (100 g) stem ginger, chopped

1. Put the garlic, salt, lemon rind and juice, sugar and vinegar in a pan, bring to the boil and simmer for 5 minutes.
2. Put the pears, onions, raisins, apples and ginger in a large china or earthenware (not metal) bowl and stir well.
3. Pour the spiced vinegar over the fruit, stir well, cover and leave for 12 hours.
4. Turn into a stainless steel, enamel or non-stick coated pan, bring slowly to the boil and boil gently for 3-4 hours, stirring frequently, until the preserve is thick and all the liquid has been absorbed.
5. Pour the chutney into warm, sterilized jars. Cover with a waxed paper disc and vinegar-proof screw-on lids (used coffee jars with plastic lids are ideal). Label, and store in a cool, dry, dark place.

Spiced Oranges

Fills two 1 lb (450 g) jars

4 large oranges, washed
¾ pt (425 ml) white distilled vinegar
8 oz (225 g) sugar
1 level tsp whole cloves

1. Put the oranges in a pan, cover with water, bring to the boil and simmer for 8-10 minutes, until the skins are tender. Drain and reserve the liquid.
2. Thickly slice the oranges and discard any pips.
3. Bring the vinegar, sugar, cloves and ¼ pt (150 ml) of the reserved liquid slowly to the boil, stirring to dissolve the sugar. Simmer for 5 minutes.
4. Add the orange slices and simmer for 20 minutes.
5. Drain the orange slices and pack them into warm, sterilized jars. Fast-boil the pickling vinegar for 10 minutes, then pour it over the oranges.
6. Leave to cool, then cover with vinegar-proof screw or clip-on lids. Store for 2 weeks before using.

Pickled Prunes

Fills three 1 lb (450 g) jars

1¼ lb (550 g) prunes
¾ pt (425 ml) tea, strained
thinly pared rind and juice of 1 lemon
thinly pared rind and juice of 1 orange
1 pt (575 ml) white distilled vinegar
1 lb (450 g) light Muscovado sugar
1 stick cinnamon

1. Soak the prunes in the tea overnight.

2. Next day, bring them slowly to the boil. Remove from heat, then cool.

3. Put lemon and orange rind and juice, vinegar, sugar and cinnamon into a stainless steel, enamel or non-stick coated pan and bring slowly to the boil, stirring to dissolve the sugar. Simmer for 5 minutes.

4. Strain the prunes, discarding the tea, and add them to the spiced vinegar. Simmer for 3 minutes.

5. Lift out the prunes with a draining spoon and pack them into warm, sterilized jars. Fast-boil the vinegar for 10 minutes.

6. Pour over the prunes, cool, then cover with vinegar-proof screw or clip-on lids. Store for 2 weeks before using.

Raspberry Vinegar

Makes about 1 pt (575 ml)

Ideally, you need a steady crop of raspberries in the garden, as this recipe uses a fresh quantity every four days for 12 days. The flavoured vinegar can be used in salad and fruit dressings. Diluted with hot water it makes a powerful combatant to winter chills.

¾ pt (425 ml) white wine vinegar
3 times 8 oz (225 g) raspberries, hulled
12 oz (350 g) sugar

1. Put the vinegar into a china or earthenware (not metal) bowl with the first 8 oz (225 g) of raspberries. Cover and leave in a cool place for 4 days.

2. Strain and discard the raspberries. Pour the vinegar over the next batch of fruit. Cover and leave for 4 days.

3. Strain off the fruit and pour the vinegar on to the third batch. Leave for a further 4 days.

4. Strain off the fruit. Put the sugar into a stainless steel, enamel or non-stick coated pan, pour on the vinegar and stir over low heat to dissolve. Bring to the boil and boil for 5 minutes, skimming off any scum that rises.

5. Pour into sterilized bottles and cover with vinegar-proof lids. Label and store. It will keep for up to 1 year.

INDEX